*Edited by Paul Herron* *Volume 8, 2011*



FRONT COVER: Anaïs Nin; photograph by Marlis Schwieger

BACK COVER: Reginald Pole.

## Editor's Note

Volume 8 of *A Café in Space* contains more revelations about Hugh Guiler, in this case his relationship with Rupert Pole. Our readers are aware that both men were married to Anaïs Nin, and from 1955 to 1966, she was married to both bigamously. Recently collected correspondence from Nin, Guiler, and Pole will, however, reveal how rapidly the dynamic of the complicated three-way relationship changed as Nin approached death, resulting in a surprising collaboration and mutual understanding between the two men afterwards.

Anaïs Nin never discussed her final illness publicly, nor did she write about it, except in her unpublished diaries *Book of Pain* and *Book of Music*. She ended her published diary on a high note, her trip to Bali in 1974, and it was shortly thereafter Nin's cancer reappeared and claimed her life after a long and terrible struggle. Many of Nin's friends rushed to help Rupert Pole care for Nin during this time, and one of them was Barbara Kraft, who tells us that Nin encouraged her to write about her death. Kraft has penned a memoir entitled *Anaïs Nin: The Last Days*, and we include an excerpt in this issue, giving us a glimpse into what was perhaps Nin's bitterest time, being robbed of life just as she was finally enjoying success and fame after decades of effort.

We also take a look at the enigmatic Reginald Pole, Rupert Pole's father, who was a renowned stage actor, writer, and director, through the eyes of an acquaintance, a lover, and his "daughter-in-law," Anaïs Nin, all of whom recognize both his genius and his dark side.

Anaïs Nin's presence in the digital book realm is rapidly increasing, as nearly all her fiction and several of her diaries are now in e-book format. Both Sky Blue Press and Houghton Mifflin Harcourt are in the process of releasing Nin titles on Kindle and other digital formats, and there is one title that encapsulates her essential work, which is *The Portable Anaïs Nin*, the first digital Nin anthology, compiled and introduced by Benjamin Franklin V. We are also in the processing of digitizing past volumes of this journal.

The Anaïs Nin Trust made its first appearance at the LA Times Festival of Books in 2010, offering for sale titles from the collection that Nin and Rupert Pole assembled at their house in Silver Lake. The Nin tent was among the more memorable at the event, complete with a fainting couch and many rare books. Tree Leyburn Wright was the driving force behind the success of the event, and all remaining titles are offered through the Trust's online bookstore, anaisnintrust.org.

Kazuko Sugisaki, who tirelessly continues to promote Nin scholarship in Japan, has spearheaded the publication of a new anthology of Nin's published and unpublished diaries. The 560 page volume will be released by Suisei-sha in the fall of 2012. Also, as a result of a gift from Sugisaki, a Kazuko Sugisaki/Anaïs Nin Scholarship Fund has been established at UCLA for undergraduate students who major in studies involving modern women writers.

Adam Barron, son of electronic music innovators Louie and Bebe Barron, has begun preparation for the re-release of a 1949 recording his parents made of Anaïs Nin reading the entire contents of *House of Incest*. The original recording is being remastered and will appear on a CD later this year. All profits will go to charity.

It should be noted here that two important figures in the Nin world have passed. Renate Druks, who was one of Nin's closest friends for many years, and an inspiration for Nin's final novel, *Collages*, died in December of 2007. Tristine Rainer brings her to life in her film treatment, "The Bohemian and the Football Player," which highlights Druks' relationship with football hero Ronnie Knox. Rose Kaufman, who was a co-screenwriter of the movie *Henry & June*, died in December of 2009. Her involvement in the film is one of the topics in Anita Jarczok's article, "Eroticizing Nin, Eroticizing Women—Philip Kaufman's *Henry & June*."

Stage plays based on Nin's life and diaries continue to be written and performed. In this issue Nin scholar Sarah Burghauser gives us her impressions of Michael Phillips' *Anaïs: An Erotic Evening with Anaïs Nin*. Doraine Poretz held a live reading of her play *Anaïs Nin: Woman of the Dream*, and plans for a full staging are being developed. David Stallings' play *Anaïs Nin Goes to Hell* is being revised and there are hopes for another run on the stage. ◈

*A Café in Space* is an annual publication, and we welcome submissions of articles or proposals having to do with Anaïs Nin and her circle. See the next page for more details.

Our web site, found at www.skybluepress.com, allows users to browse the contents of past issues of this publication. Our blog (http://anaisninblog.skybluepress.com) is a place where readers can browse or make contributions. It is our sincere hope that with the journal, blog and web site we will be able to form a "café" in which Nin scholars, readers, and those with parallel interests will gather. Nin study is hampered by a lack of communication between those of us who engage in it, and this is a way to address the problem. We encourage you to "spread the word" so that we can build a strong central base of Nin scholarship and readership.

*Acknowledgements*

The Editor would like to thank the following for their assistance in the realization of this issue:

The Anaïs Nin Trust for permissions to use quotations from Anaïs Nin's work, and for photographic material.

Marlis Schwieger for permission to use her photograph of Anaïs Nin on the cover.

Michael Phillips for materials and tickets for *Anaïs: An Erotic Evening with Anaïs Nin.*

Barbara Stuhlmann for her encouragement and guidance.

Sara Herron, without whom none of this would be possible.

*A Café in Space: the Anaïs Nin Literary Journal* is published annually by Sky Blue Press, and edited by Paul Herron.



Submissions or proposals should be directed to Sky Blue Press, P.O. Box 691308, San Antonio, TX 78269 USA. Material may also be submitted by attaching a Word document to an e-mail message sent to skybluepress@skybluepress.com. Please identify the contents in the subject line or it will not be opened.

E-mail us if you wish information in order to send materials through the mail. Any unsolicited material will not be returned without inclusion of a self-stamped and addressed envelope. Safety of manuscripts and other materials is not the responsibility of Sky Blue Press.

ISBN-10: 0-9774851-7-X
ISBN-13: 978-0-9774851-7-8

Sky Blue Press
San Antonio, TX

*Barbara Kraft*

## Anaïs Nin: The Last Days

*A preface and excerpt from a new memoir*

 *writer is in the end not his books, but his myth. And that myth is in the keeping of others*—V.S. Naipaul

*Preface*

"Barbara—This is Anaïs Nin speaking. I have read your work and I think it is very good. We have many affinities. I would like you to come and see me." That was how it began. Three years later it ended in a faint whisper: "I can't tell the world about my illness, but you can, Barbara, and I want the world to know. I want you to write about this."

I have chosen to reveal the intimacies of Anaïs's last days as I witnessed them so that the story of her death is not lost. There is no such thing as death. Everything comes back in the mind's eye. Everything comes back in the crucible of the heart. She remains in my psyche all these years later as the most refined and rarified human being I have ever encountered. As Marcel Proust observed, "People do not die immediately for us, but remain bathed in a sort of aura of life...it is as though they were traveling abroad."

I met Anaïs Nin February 8, 1974. I know the exact date because it is the first entry in the diary I began to keep that day under her guidance...

"I met with Miss Nin today. It was as if I had always known her, so easy was the dialogue and yet I was conscious of being in the company of a vital presence. In a strange way I feel as if my life has been a preparation for this meeting with this singularly, uncommon woman..."

This situation came about through the auspices of International College in Los Angeles, a tutorial college of scholars and professionals whose roster at the time included Anaïs Nin, Buckminster Fuller and Lawrence Durrell. Two and a half years later, my diary, *The Restless Spirit: Journal of a Gemini*, was published by Celestial Arts/Les Femmes with a preface by Anaïs.

From the moment of our initial meeting until her death in January 1977 I was captivated by Anaïs, who inspired intense feelings in everyone she came in contact with. No one was left untouched by an encounter with the woman her brother Joaquín referred to as the "steel hummingbird." It was either love or hate. For me it was love at first sight.

When she answered the door that balmy February afternoon, the kind we Californians are known to brag about, I was mesmerized by the figure who greeted me. She was Henry Miller's "Être Étoilique." Dressed in a floor-length, gauzy, cerise-hued Indian gown—the kind popular among the counterculture in those days but one which she wore regally—she was taller than I had imagined. Perhaps five feet six inches. Her center-parted hair sat on top of her head like a tiny golden crown. There was not a line on the finely-wrought, mother-of-pearl skin to indicate her seventy-some years. She was poetry embodied with a hauntingly accented, slightly husky, flute-like voice. As she led me into the house, I followed in her wake, feeling awkward and ungainly while she seemed to glide over the rose-colored carpet like a swan skimming the surface of still water.

Throughout 1974, we met nearly every week and during those sessions I would read to her from the diary that I was writing. It was the story of my life as I lived it from day to day between our meetings in Anaïs's glass "house of mirrors" overlooking Silver Lake. She shared the house with her long-time companion Rupert Pole, who built the house for her. Anaïs never articulated exactly what her relationship to Pole was, and I never asked. He came and went, fetched the mail, cleaned the pool, offered a glass of wine. Husband or companion? At the time, it didn't matter, and I paid scant attention to him that first year.

The tutorial relationship between us quickly turned into an intimacy. This gift for intimacy with those whom Anaïs perceived as like-spirits, or would convert into like-spirits, was one of her most prominent traits; her work reverberates with references to twin-ship, sisterhood, and like-hood.

At the end of that first year, December of 1974, Anaïs was hospitalized with advanced cancer. A lengthy and devastating surgery followed. For the next two years she was in and out of the hospital for repeated sessions of chemotherapy, radiation, and additional surgeries. The golden crown fell out in clumps on the bathroom floor, and she was attached, through an incision on her right side, to a series of bags that contained the bilious, acidic fluids draining from her broken body. These years of pain and suffering carved her a new face and rendered her a mortal being, made of flesh and bones and blood. As her illness progressed, my visits became more frequent. During the last six months of her life I went to see her as often as I could, usually three or four times a week; when I was unable to visit we spoke on the phone.

To participate in Nin's death was an extraordinary experience. There was the time shortly before she died when my phone rang late at night. "Barbara, do you think you could slip away for a bit? I know it is terribly late, but I cannot bear the pain anymore. Please come and sit with me. I need you."

When I arrived she was in terrible distress and asked if I would get in bed with her and hold her in my arms. She said, "I've never done this before. I've never wept on another woman's shoulder. But there are some places where women touch that men cannot know."

When she died January 14, 1977, Anaïs Nin was 73 years old. She so wanted to live, this graceful, elegant, cultivated woman whom Henry Miller called "a masterpiece."

Illness is the great leveler from which none of us is immune. It flushes out all the old, buried truths and puts us in touch with the essential meaning of things. There is no time, no energy for masks, veils, labyrinths, interior cities or multiple hearts. Death hovered over her, a falcon circling its prey; it was the one reality that Anaïs could not transcend or transmute or transform or levitate with the magic of words. It was a reality she met with a dignity that tore at the heart of all of us who knew her and were close to her. No one dies as Anaïs did. During this time I learned that the essence of a human being is resistant to time and that, in spite of all, it is possible for human beings to find grace.

Several years later I met Henry Miller, and we reminisced fondly about Anaïs. (Ironically, he too was nearing the end.) Lovers during the 1930s in Paris when both were struggling to make names for themselves, their paths crossed one last time when they ended up in the same hospital at the same time, separated by a floor or two.

Leaning on his elbows across the dinner table one evening, Henry laughed as he told me that Anaïs was the "greatest fabulist" he had ever known, and one also possessed of the nine lives of the cat. Henry was a tough old bird, rather like a turkey, with his croaky voice, heavily veined hands, parchment-thin skin, wattled throat and naked head. The memory of Anaïs's shenanigans amused him, spreading across his wrinkled face in a broad smile. Being of a less sanguine disposition than Miller, Anaïs herself referred to her lies as "mensonges vitals" by which she meant "the lies which give life."

As I was to learn shortly before her death and quite by accident, Anaïs had been married to two men at the same time. I was in New York visiting a friend when one of Nin's acquaintances invited me to a dinner being given by an Ian Hugo. It was then that I learned that Ian Hugo was Anaïs' husband Hugh Guiler, not Rupert Pole.

Nin married Hugh Guiler in 1923, met Rupert Pole in 1947 (he was 16 years her junior), and married him bigamously in 1955. Once her diaries were published, she was forced to annul the Pole marriage for tax reasons. Her legal husband was and remained Hugh Guiler until the end of her life, while Rupert Pole, her constant companion, cared for and nursed her through her long and terrible battle with cancer.

A myth in her own time, the Scheherazade of the diary genre, both of her husbands "spared" her life, and by so doing made her creative life possible. Without their support there would not have been the Anaïs Nin of the diaries as we know her. When she died the obituaries in the East listed Hugh P. Guiler as the husband of the deceased; in the West, Rupert Pole.

The publication of Nin's diaries fortuitously coincided with the women's movement, which catapulted her into the status of an icon. She was thought by her followers to possess an authentic feminine voice, free of male influence. She presented herself as having successfully defied the conventions of a woman's role, emerging unscathed to tell the tale. It was an unbeatable combination in those idealistic days.

My personal experience with Nin is where I started, but I'll never know how much of what she related to me about her actual life was true and how much was her "signature" evasive fabrication. In the 1990s two biographies appeared revealing that Nin's published diaries were all smoke and veils; that her life as she wrote about it in the diaries was a labyrinth of lies which she edited and rewrote in a never ending re-creation of self. (I reviewed the Deidre Bair biography for the Los Angeles Times in 1995.) There is no mention in the published diaries of her bicoastal husbands, of her incestuous relationship with her father, published posthumously as *Incest* by Rupert Pole, of her many abortions.

Does it matter? It can be argued that there is no language without deceit. The diaries are, in a sense, an imagined version of Nin's life as she wanted us to perceive it; perhaps how she herself wanted to perceive it. My feeling upon our initial meeting was of a woman who had fashioned herself to become the myth of her own design.

In retrospect, I have come think of her as like the Sirens of mythology. Part bird, part woman, they lured the sailors to their deaths on the rocky coasts they inhabited. There was something in Nin's voice, in the timbre, in her articulation that lured her followers, that lured me, into the intoxicating aura of her being. Odysseus, warned by Circe of the power of the Sirens, wisely stuffed his ears with wax and had himself tied to the mast of his ship before it sailed past the Siren's craggy home. As Edmund Wilson, one of Anaïs's *en passant* lovers wryly observed, she was both a "practical little Franco-Spanish housewife" and a "lovely little nymph who was not quite a human being."

In the end, her spirit transcended her human failings. We should all be able to say as much. She was the physical embodiment of poetic lyricism, and in this role, in the role of the creative spirit, she spread light and hope. That is how she will be remembered; that is how I remember her.

## *Chapter 1*

The day it all began was cold and chilly. The sky bore down a monotonous grey. Even the trees were limp and depressed. Christmas seemed remote. Not just one day away. As I drove down the steep driveway to the house nestled at the bottom I saw Anaïs standing there waiting for me. A slight figure in the dampness. It was odd. She had never come out to meet me before. She must have been listening for the car.

I gathered up the flowers I had stopped to buy on the way over and opened the door of the car holding them out to her. Ignoring them or perhaps not seeing them, she began to speak in her carefully modulated voice.

"We cannot work today, Barbara. I called you but you had already left. I spoke to your husband. He said you had just left. I'm very sorry that you came all this way for nothing. Rupert took me to the doctor's this morning and they are putting me in the hospital tomorrow morning for tests.

"On Christmas Day?" I asked.

"Yes. They say it can't wait."

"But why? What's wrong?"

"It's the cancer again."

She spoke dispassionately, uttering the word "cancer" as if it was simply something to be dealt with as efficiently and as quickly as possible. Her attitude suggested a passing inconvenience, not much more than an unexpected trip to the dentist.

"Luckily vaginal cancer is the easiest kind to control. At least we know now. The not knowing is always so terrible. But it will be fine. I have had this twice before. Both times in New York. But you must not worry about me. I have complete faith in my doctors."

The twist of her reddish gold hair glowed like a small crown on top of her head. Stunned, I focused on that to avoid looking at her face. What could I say that would match her equanimity?

In a wistful voice she added, "Isn't that strange—to go into the hospital on Christmas Day? You know, when I was a child, I was very ill one year at Christmas. I nearly died. I was nine years old at the time. My father left us a few months after that. I have never liked Christmas.

"Rupert and I have to see the family today and do some errands this afternoon... This has all been so sudden. We weren't prepared for it. I want to live. I have a great deal to live for. I have many things yet to write."

I didn't want to think about her words, only the sound of her voice. It was like listening to the middle range of a flute. Beautiful and flowing.

"This tomorrow is for tests and to decide upon the treatment. I will call and let you know what they decide to do...if we had time I would ask you in for a cup of tea, but we have to leave immediately. You must continue to write. You must work well until we can meet again. Call Rupert. He will let you know what they find. Maybe it will be nothing. At least we will know. I have so much to live for. Continue to work, Barbara. You must write. We will work again when I get home."

I marveled at her control. It was not human. Was it possible that she could be so calm, so courteous, so concerned about me and my little scribblings? How did she really feel? Was this a pose for me or for her or for both of us? Was she really so cavalier, so brave, so pure of spirit? I was startled at her words because it was the first time she had ever said anything intimate to me—other than at our initial meeting when she had spoken to me about her father. I never thought of her as having mortal feelings because she appeared perfect, and that perfection made her remote. She walked in an aura of noli me tangere—"touch me not!"

Tears gathered in the corner of my eyes and I struggled to hold them back. What would I do without her? How would I go on, having barely started? Suddenly, standing there in the cold greyness and the dripping trees, I recalled that she had complained of stomach pain and not being able to hold anything down on several occasions over the past few months. Her mildly expressed discomfort had not registered in my consciousness because I had been so involved in my own problems—problems that I passionately recorded in my diary day in, day out, and then read to her at our weekly meetings.

*I looked at you then directly for the first time, Anaïs. It was something I could no longer avoid doing. I had avoided looking at you because I did not want to penetrate the carefully placed mask that was getting you, me, through this meeting. Masks are like manners. They give us a form with which to deal with the unspeakable. When our eyes did meet, you suddenly seemed small and slight and frail. You were not a myth, a muse, a goddess, a literary legend floating in a dramatic swirl of black cape captured for posterity in a famed photo by the famous Jill Krementz.*

*Shivering in the damp cold, you were a woman wearing an old, out of style black knit dress with a short white jacket thrown over her shoulders and you had cancer and you were going into the hospital on Christmas Day to be examined and probed and handled and tested and hopefully treated. At the same time there was an agelessness about you, one which you never lost despite all that you were to endure over the next two years.*

*We embraced one another carefully. I held out the flowers. Purple and magenta and lavender flowers—all your favorite colors. You took them but said nothing. I don't think you really saw them. It was the only indication of how upset you must have been. Before going back into the house you told me, once again, that I should call Rupert.*

"He will let you know what they find. Maybe it will be nothing. At least we will know. I have so much to live for. Continue to work, Barbara. You must write. And when I get home we will work together again."

With that she turned away and walked back to the house. Her image dissolved blurring in front of me into a black flame tipped with gold like an El Greco painting. I got back into my bright, little car. It was a little yellow Porsche which I dearly loved. I tend to drive fast but that day I drove home slowly.

*It was sprinkling when Rupert took you to the hospital the next day. I could just imagine the halls decorated with tinsel and somewhere an artificial tree and Christmas cards dangling on a slack string strung under a doorway. How depressing you must have found it.*

*At home I went through the tired ritual of cooking Christmas dinner for family and friends. We were twelve around the table. My husband, my ten-year-old daughter Jennifer, my two step-sons, my mother, my father, and my three sisters. I can't recall who else was there. I looked across the length of the table at my husband carving the turkey, at my father working his napkin into the collar of his shirt, at my mother picking up her fork, examining it and, from the expression on her face, approving the gleaming sterling which had been polished for the occasion earlier, I looked at them and saw the remnants of a life I was no longer living. It was not their fault. It was I who had changed. And, you, Anaïs, were the impetus of that change.*

*By the time everyone left the day's drizzle had turned into a deluge, lashing out against the ceiling to floor glass doors of the house, scarring them with deep slashes that bled down the glass in waves. Doing the dishes I thought of you lying in the hospital. Was the same rain beating against your windows? Were you alone or was Rupert still with you? What would these tests reveal? How long would they take? Would we really meet and work again?*

A week later I heard from Anaïs. It was late in the afternoon and the January sun squatted on the horizon like a blazing temple. Listening to her words, I watched as it slipped over the edge of the world.

"Barbara, this is Anaïs." Her lilting, slow-paced voice startled me. Every syllable so clear, so perfectly articulated. I had expected a call from Rupert, not from her.

"I tried to phone you earlier today but there was no answer. I promised I would phone you when we knew something definite. I am to have surgery Thursday morning."

Then she said, "We need eight units of blood. I have a very rare blood type. A-negative. When we got home Rupert took charge and began telephoning our friends asking them to donate blood. I objected to this and then it occurred to him to call the Women's Building, where I have spoken many times. I told Rupert that I would call you myself in case you might know of anyone who might be able to donate a unit."

"I don't know what type I have, Anaïs, but I'll find out first thing in the morning." Eight units of blood seemed like an awful lot of blood for a woman who weighed barely 100 pounds.

"Oh no, not you," she protested. "You're too slight. You have to weigh a certain amount, and I know you are not heavy enough. But if you have a friend it doesn't have to be the same type as mine. They have a blood bank that they draw upon. I have to replace the units that we use. Rupert is going to ask at the Women's Building as well. Stay in touch with Rupert. Call Rupert."

A few days later I went to give blood as I was not as slight as Anaïs supposed, weighing 112 pounds, two pounds over the mandatory 110. As she was inserting the IV into my left arm, the nurse in charge told me that there had been a steady stream of women all day long and the previous day as well. A pleasant, middle-aged woman, she was perplexed at the turnout.

"I've never seen anything like it," she said. "Such an odd assortment of women of all ages. Some looked like flowers in long madras dresses and beads and feathers and others in blue jeans and t-shirt and combat boots. You know the type, the raggedy libbers who go braless and don't shave their legs. It was a carnival in here yesterday. All for this woman writer on the third floor. I can't remember her name. It has a foreign sound to it. Is she a friend of yours? Who is she, anyway? What's so special about her? Is she famous? I've never seen a turnout like this before for anyone, and I have been a nurse for fifteen years, ten in this hospital, and we get a lot of celebrities here."

*Lying there that day, glancing up now and again at the bag dangling overhead slowly filling with my blood, I remembered my first visit to you, a year earlier almost to the day.*

*You opened the door wearing one of your long flowing dresses, your little white poodle Piccolino barking and jumping all over the place. You had the body, the walk, the spirit of a girl. We sat in your small, book-lined study, the shelves stacked with volumes of the "Diary" in English and various translations, our knees touching for lack of space, and discovered "our many affinities," to use your phrase.*

*There was our mutual interest in women such as George Sand and Lou Andreas-Salomé. I told you that I had written a radio play on Salomé, and some months later, when you were asked to write a preface for a biography on her, we discussed her life and relationships with Nietzsche, Rilke and Freud, and you quoted a passage from my play.*

*We shared Catholic backgrounds, I more comfortably than you, and musical ones as well. Your father had been a concert pianist and composer and I had been a piano major on scholarship in an all-girl's Catholic college. You were amused when I told you that it was there that I met my husband, who had been one of my instructors in the music department. There were only two or three men on the faculty in those days and he was one of them. An adjunct professor, he taught percussion at the school (as music majors we were required to have a working knowledge of all the instruments in an orchestra); his main job was with the Los Angeles Philharmonic, where he played percussion. He was also a gifted composer although at the time that we met he had not yet received the recognition that would come later. To my parents' dismay, he was also Jewish, 20 years older than I, and divorced with two small children.*

*As the afternoon light narrowed that first day in your monastic little writing cell, you spoke to me about your father as if he were still alive and a part of your daily existence. You told me how the diary began as a letter to your father, and in that moment you were a young girl all over again, your voice full of pain, reliving for how many times the abandonment of your father. It was a discordant note in the peace and serenity you exuded. The timbre of your voice was plaintive and hollow, and later that night when I was recording our meeting in the pages of my nascent diary, the image that came to mind was the desolate sound of a metal fitting striking a flagpole in the dark swirl of a windy, starless night.*

*The talk about your father made me uncomfortable. I was startled and pulled back a bit. It seemed odd for a woman of your age to be revisiting the past with such pained intimacy in the company of a virtual stranger, and I felt a prick of doubt as to the stability of the woman I was about to become involved with. It wasn't what you said, but rather how you said it. There was a moment then when I wanted to leave; it frightened me that you were so involved with a past so far removed, and I wasn't certain whether I wanted to stay. Something wasn't quite right. But I put this uneasiness out of my mind and saw instead only what you wanted me to see, which matched perfectly with what I wanted to see—for the stronger sensation was that of being transported to another world, to the realm of the possibility of things becoming.*

*From the first, I perceived of you as someone unpossessible, ephemeral, forever beyond my grasp, and yet someone who reached out and shook hands with my soul. There are encounters in which all that can be known is known, and this was such an encounter. Implicit in our meeting was my unconditional acceptance of you as you presented yourself. All those craggy places where we one day might collide were left on the doorstep of your hillside home like the rattler's shed skin. While we had many affinities, instinctively, I knew even then, although I ignored it, that we were fundamentally very different women with very different values.*

*The strange thing is that before meeting you, I was only mildly interested in your work. I was not a fan and actually had read very little of it, and what I had read had not compelled me. I was at loose ends and looking for a direction when a friend gave me a brochure she had received announcing that you were teaching privately through an organization called International College. I thought, "Why not?"*

*I phoned the college and was told to submit some work which they would pass on to you. I sent a radio play which had recently received a national award. It was based on the life of Maud Gonne, the Irish actress, revolutionary and extravagant, if reluctant, muse who haunted the poetry of William Butler Yeats. No two women could have been more diametrically different than you and the pistol-toting, six-foot-tall Maud Gonne, first woman to be a member of the IRA.*

*A few weeks later, in early January, the phone rang. I remember the time quite distinctly. It was seven p.m., and I was in the midst of a heated argument with my husband. I picked up the phone and heard your voice for the first time, a voice unlike any I had ever heard before or since.*

*"Barbara—this is Anaïs Nin speaking. I have read your work and I think it is very good. We have many affinities. I would like you to come and see me."* ◈

## Rupert Pole and Hugh Guiler

*An unlikely partnership**

When Anaïs Nin became seriously ill with the last bout of cancer that would ultimately take her life, she was in Los Angeles with her lover of nearly thirty years, Rupert Pole. Nin's relationship with her legal husband, Hugh Guiler, who was in New York, had deteriorated to the point where she struggled with the idea of even being with him for short periods of time, and she sought a way out of the relationship. Her illness, while providing a valid reason for not traveling to New York, also forced her to face the truth: she felt the need to put an end to her guilt-ridden commitment to Guiler, which, she was convinced, was hindering her ability to recover. Illness also forced her, as we shall see, to be truthful to Pole about the fact she had been living a double life, dividing her time between the two men for many years. The events just before and after Nin's death would ultimately bring Pole and Guiler, seemingly shrouded in secrecy for decades, together to form a most unlikely alliance.

Nin's feelings were sometimes expressed to the analyst she and Guiler had shared in New York, Dr. Inge Bogner. In the following letter, Nin describes her growing realization that she must somehow free herself from Guiler:

*May 4, 1975*

Dear Inge: I suffered a real block in writing until this week. I thought I had lost my power. This is overcome now and I am at work again. But as for writing you I realize it was because I had *too much* to tell you. I will try. The surgery predictions were so solemn, the concern of the surgeons so obvious, the pain so great, that I felt I was facing the possibility of death. At the same time Rupert's love and determination that I should live, the wholeness of his love, and my need to unburden myself, my need of his support and taking over small things, like the key to my post office box, which brought on a total confusion. His attitude was perfect. He understood the motivation for the double life. I never realized the weight of this burden until I suddenly shed it. He accepted the responsibilities. I did not, could not conceal my mailing of Hugo's monthly income. I could telephone Hugo. In millions of ways Rupert was there. Under the influence of Demerol, great pain and great weakness, I told Rupert everything, but what frightened me was my

---

* *Commentary by the editor.*

open rebellion against Hugo, my feeling I no longer wanted to return to him, that the double life was the cause of stress, that to tell Rupert the truth suddenly made me feel whole and at peace, able to put all my strength on getting well… During that entire period Rupert threw all his energy, his devotion, his faith into the fight. He came four times a day [to the hospital]. But what a relief to lean, to confide, to trust. So much of my strength went into forcing myself to return to Hugo. I was shocked by the total break in myself, the admission I would never make. I did not want to see Hugo. I felt him merely as a burden. I felt we were bad for each other. Of course, the relief, the absence of tension was a help in the struggle for health… I feel completely detached from Hugo. I miss our talks with you. I want to know how Hugo feels. The last time we spent together in Paris he dragged his depression, his total absence of livingness and made my task heavier. He was like a dead weight. I was already in pain getting through my interviews with pain killers. When someone complimented him on the humor in his films he wrote to me: "And I see myself as a sad sack."

Please tell me if Hugo is taking the long time lapse well. I wish he would admit he is happier without me. Friends tell me he is better when I am not there. I feel he is, towards me, in a perpetual sulk resenting the past. I don't blame him. I don't think in terms of blame of either one of us. We were unsuited for each other. Because he was not alive I sought life elsewhere. Because of my behavior, he was depressed. I have to wait until the end of treatment. Then I will come to NY and face the situation. When Rupert accepted all I had done and interpreted it as wanting to protect him and Hugo, he also expects me to put an end to this situation. I am not physically ready to face the results of my ending the double life.

For the first time in my life, living one life, one love, reveals a peace I never knew, an absence of strain I never knew.

My love and gratitude—A

Several months later, after having written, but not having sent, a letter to Hugo requesting his release of her, Nin again wrote to Bogner:

*December 20, 1975*

Dear Inge: What I have to write you about is not new for you but it has become critical. You know how many years you worked to eradicate my sense of guilt towards Hugo. Once I said to you: "What would happen if I stayed away completely?" You answered: "Knowing you, you could not live with your guilt."

The subject has come up again when I met a Dr. Brugh Joy. A year and a half ago, he quit a promising doctor's practice. He went to the

East. He returned a mystic who had cured himself of an illness and discovered he had strong healing powers. He came to see me. He read the diaries before coming and had the instant intuition: too much giving, tendency to sacrifice, guilt. Yesterday he brought [a tape recording of] the talk on the meaning of cancer. Possibly an obstacle to growth and freedom, a growth gone wrong. Martyrdom? No, I said, no martyrdom, but sacrifice and guilt.

But I had guilt for being happy, when Hugo was handicapped and felt a sense of failure. As you know, instinctively, when I was very ill, I wrote you I could not return to Hugo. You suggested I wait until I could come to NY.

When I was ill I felt Hugo was the source of my illness. That it was like a life long stress, effort, deception and unhappiness. We are never at peace or happy together. I wrote many times: he is my burden—he is a thorn in my side. The conflict between compassion and the need to be free.

Dr. Joy feels I may not get well until I let go of this. That I weaken and overprotect Hugo, that I don't let him go. Will he let me go? Should I ask him to come and see me? Should I let you tell him?

It is now a matter of my survival. I don't want a divorce. I don't want people to know. I want nothing injurious to him. I want no recriminations—a loving, warm separation, and when I'm well I will visit him.—Anaïs

Still, there was no concrete answer to Nin's plea for separate lives. In August of 1976, Guiler was facing a hernia surgery in New York, alone, and, perhaps partly out of compassion and partly out of guilt, Nin made sure Guiler had a private room and nurse, and she dutifully called him twice every day. In the meantime, Pole, who was now aware of the situation in New York, generously previewed Guiler's newest film, *Luminescence*, with Anaïs, which resulted in the following letter from Nin to Guiler, written August 13, 1976:

Darling:

Seeing the film twice was a good suggestion as I had missed the theme. The effects are always poetic, and rich, full of surprises, many dimensional. The film has marvelous colors and much animation. It is a development of your visionary power. It achieves more than an animated painting because there is beauty in the mobility, in the games with shadows and surprising new evolutions.

You are no doubt the filmmaker of the dream and vision. The images remain with one for a long time.

Anaïs

Finally, in October of 1976, Nin learned that Bogner had spoken with Guiler, and that he had agreed that it was best that he and Nin lead separate lives. While Nin's sense of oppressive guilt was finally lifted, the reprieve would be brief—she would die three months later.

After Nin's death on January 14, 1977, her obituary in *The New York Times* listed Hugh Guiler as her surviving husband, while in Los Angeles, the survivor was Rupert Pole. Since the two of them now had a common interest in sorting out Nin's affairs, estate, and ongoing publications, Guiler was prompted to write the following handwritten letter to Pole, date February 23, 1977:

Apartment 14B
3 Washington Square Village
New York, NY 10012

Dear Rupert:

As we are going to be communicating with each other from now on I think it is well that I do what I can to make things as easy as possible for us both, and I want to start by being quite frank with you.

First, I have been quite aware for more than ten years of your special relationship with Anaïs and I want you to know that I have not only respected that, but have been, and am grateful to you for having made her last years happy. There was a tacit understanding between Anaïs and me during those years, that we would allow each other to lead relatively independent lives and that this would in no way alter the deep devotion we felt towards each other, a devotion that became even stronger towards the end.

I am also grateful for all the help you gave Anaïs during her long illness. I wanted to share this burden with you, but Anaïs told me that my health would have broken down if I had attempted to do this.

In the light of the above I hope you will feel at ease in communicating directly with me from now on.

Sincerely yours,
Hugo

Pole's response is preserved in the form of a draft handwritten in pencil.

My Dear Hugo

Please forgive a typewritten letter but my handwriting (never very legible) became completely illegible during Anaïs's illness.

I am so grateful for your letter initiating our correspondence. I understand now why Anaïs loved and worshipped you so deeply. I cannot think of anything that would please Anaïs more than our close, sympathetic cooperation to carry on her work.

It has helped me greatly to recall an incident I'm sure you remember. In '66 Anaïs was in the hospital in NY facing surgery. The galleys of Diary 1 were brought to her and she prayed that she might live long enough to know the reaction to her Diary. The gods granted her with 10 years—years of fulfillment as an artist—years in which she was able to carry on a love affair with the world through the lectures and correspondence.

I am sending you a book *Life after Life* which more than any other convinced Anaïs that death is a joyous experience and helped so much prepare her for her "promotion to another realm."

The tribute here* was just the right mood. There was a soft jazz combo with Cuban drums and bamboo wind chimes that would have delighted Anaïs. The University is making a tape and I will send you a copy as soon as it is completed. I have [heard wonderful things] of your program from Sharon [Spencer], John F[errone] and Joaquin. People were particularly awed at hearing Anaïs's voice in your beautiful film.†

I will send an inventory of Anaïs's possessions as soon as I can manage it. In the meantime please rest assured that everything is insured and that nothing will be changed in my lifetime. The house will be kept as a working studio to carry on the writing. Right now I am drowned in work: getting materials ready for UCLA, for John Ferrone's memorial photo book (pictures of Anaïs), the Childhood Diary (the excellent translation is justified—Anaïs said: "I can't believe I didn't write it in English"); Joaquin will write the preface; Diary 7 (from 1966 to the present); and finally the '20s period from the end of the childhood Diary when Anaïs was 17 to 1931, the beginning of Vol. 1.

I suggested to John Ferrone that only you should write the preface for this diary. You are both the central figure and hero of this period. I hope you will accept.‡

Hugo, I know that you have moments of unbearable loneliness, as I do. It helps me to recall a line from the Bali diary (Anaïs wrote this as an ending for Diary 7):

---

* Pole is referring to a tribute service for Nin in Los Angeles on her birthday, Feb. 21, 1977.

† This is a reference to a similar New York service, held Feb. 22, 1977, at which Guiler's film *Bells of Atlantis* was screened.

‡ While Guiler agreed in principle, it was Nin's brother Joaquín who wrote the prefaces for each of the *Early Diaries*.

*Let me think of death as the Balinese do, as a flight to another life, a joyous transformation, a release of our spirit so it might visit all other lives.*

In these moments remember Anaïs's spirit is now free—free to be with you whenever you need her.
With profound sympathy,
Rupert

Guiler's response:

*March 10, 1977*

Dear Rupert,

I have received the book you were kind enough to send me—*Life After Life*—and I want to thank you. It happens that I had read it, at the suggestion of Dr. Inge Bogner, but I am glad to have another copy, as I have been lending it to friends. I found it fascinating, and am particularly glad that Anaïs also read it, and I can understand how it must have contributed to her peaceful and even joyous acceptance at the end.

Thank you also for telling me about the success of the tribute in L.A. We here are hoping soon to receive the figures of the financial results which the V.P. of New York University has requested before he can recommend the plan for a *public* showing, maybe at Town Hall, which they are willing to consider financing, so I would appreciate your either giving this information to Joaquin, or calling me direct: in A.M. 212-344-3010 10-12 noon, otherwise 212-254-4096.

I also appreciate your suggestion that I write the preface for the Anaïs diary to 1931 and will see how John Ferrone feels about this.

I do feel Anaïs's presence more than ever.
Yours,
Hugo

P.S. Perhaps you will give me the telephone numbers where I can reach you.

Guiler and Pole continued their collaboration throughout 1977, and indeed, until the end of Guiler's life in 1985. In December 1977, Guiler sent a Christmas card to Pole, and the handwritten text is as follows:

Dear Rupert: Thank you for your beautiful greeting card, your words, and particularly for the photo of Anaïs with its fine quote of her words. This photo is, of course, the one that appears in the book about the Snyder film. If you are in touch with him could you perhaps ask him if he would give me permission to use the shot very briefly in a new short 16mm film I am planning. It will not be about Anaïs in any way, but I can see it as a part of an incidental short sequence inspired by Raymond Moody's *Life After Life*, which you sent me.

And, by the way, if you can get any time from your overburdened days, could you send me a list of Anaïs's books at the house. I suppose they are safely locked up behind glass and so protected from passing visitors, but I might like to choose some of them for my own reading.

I agree with you that if we can survive 1977, we can go through anything, so I feel confident in wishing you the best for the New Year.
Affectionately,
Hugo ◈

APARTMENT 14B
3 WASHINGTON SQUARE VILLAGE
NEW YORK, N. Y. 10012

FEBRUARY 23, 1977

DEAR RUPERT:

AS WE ARE GOING TO BE COMMUNICATING WITH EACH OTHER FROM NOW ON I THINK IT IS WELL THAT I DO WHAT I CAN TO MAKE THINGS AS EASY AS POSSIBLE FOR US BOTH, AND I WANT TO START BY BEING QUITE FRANK WITH YOU.

FIRST, I HAVE BEEN QUITE AWARE FOR MORE THAN TEN YEARS OF YOUR SPECIAL RELATIONSHIP WITH ANAIS AND I WANT YOU TO KNOW THAT I HAVE NOT ONLY RESPECTED THAT, BUT HAVE BEEN, AND AM GRATEFUL TO YOU FOR HAVING MADE HER LAST YEARS HAPPY. THERE WAS A TACIT UNDERSTANDING BETWEEN ANAIS AND ME DURING THOSE YEARS, THAT WE WOULD ALLOW EACH OTHER TO LEAD RELATIVELY INDEPENDENT LIVES AND THAT THIS WOULD IN NO WAY ALTER THE DEEP DEVOTION WE FELT TOWARDS EACH OTHER,— A DEVOTION WHICH BECAME EVEN STRONGER TOWARDS THE END.

I AM ALSO GRATEFUL FOR ALL THE HELP YOU GAVE ANAIS DURING HER LONG ILLNESS. I WANTED TO SHARE THIS BURDEN WITH YOU, BUT ANAIS TOLD ME THAT MY HEALTH WOULD HAVE BROKEN DOWN IF I HAD ATTEMPTED TO DO THIS.

IN THE LIGHT OF THE ABOVE I HOPE YOU WILL FEEL AT EASE IN COMMUNICATING DIRECTLY WITH ME FROM NOW ON.

SINCERELY YOURS,

Hugo

*Ian Hugo*

## The Making of *Bells of Atlantis*

*A lecture*[*]

Thank you for your kind response, which I am sure is also meant as a tribute to Anaïs Nin. I do think that this film does bring her closer to you—to her style as a poetic writer of the first order, and her presence as an extraordinarily sensitive and warm human being. I can certainly testify personally to this through the almost 54 years that we were married, to the time of her death in January of this year.[†]

And I will add that her physical beauty seemed to glow as if from some inner light which, as I now see more clearly, enabled her to explore, day by day, "the lost continent in ourselves" (a phrase by the poet Marianne Moore in referring to "Bells of Atlantis").

And it is only now that I fully realize how much I owed to her presence and her encouragement all those years in trying to explore my own "lost continent," which I first tried to reach out to in making this film.

In 1950, after the release of my first film *Ai-Ye*, a poetic documentary shot near Acapulco, in Mexico, I felt there was a wide field for the enhancement of written poetry through motion and color. My wife, ~~Anaïs Nin, recently deceased~~, had at that time completed what I considered, and still consider her most inspired work: *House of Incest*, a prose poem. It presented a great challenge...I was eager to make the attempt, not with the whole long poem, but with a few selected passages.

I was determined to avoid the mistake of trying to make a literal translation from words into film, and so...in that primitive Mexican environment, and inspired by the poem, with the feeling that I was about to descend into mysterious yet strangely familiar deep sea caverns...I waited for the dream to lead me where it would. And this actually happened.

---

[*] *The lecture was delivered after the screening of* Bells of Atlantis *at the American Film Festival on May 27, 1977. This text is taken directly from Hugh Guiler's notes, a copy of which he sent to Rupert Pole. Handwritten cross-outs and corrections are maintained in this version—Ed.*

[†] *One of the attendees reports that there was an "audible gasp" at the mention of marriage to Nin, perhaps because of the belief that, as noted in the* Diary *and past joint presentations, their relationship was purely professional—Ed.*

On our next trip to Acapulco, Anaïs and I were walking along the beach and suddenly came upon an old sea vessel half buried in the sand, its hull exposed, the curved ribs jutting up above the sand and one porthole like an eye looking in and out.

We both had the same thought almost simultaneously: "This is the womb...and here is the location for the film."

I had my camera with me and at once, holding it by hand, as I usually do, I started filming...I filmed in the rhythm of my breathing...something that at that time only a 16mm camera, or a smaller one, could do.

Shortly afterward, we returned to the hull with a white silk hammock we had bought at the marketplace. We hung this between two of the ribs and I shot Anaïs swinging gently in the hammock. Then...while she stood upright and held the hammock as it swung back and forth in the wind...I shot not her body, but the shadow of her body on the hammock.

With these shots as an anchor, we walked further on along the beach and came upon a large plank jutting out of the sand... A little further on there was another wreck with a series of protruding planks. In the film these planks punctuate the loud storm sequence, and the single plank in the sand became the cross behind which Anaïs stands with her hands held out horizontally.

Most of these shots were, as you have seen, superimposed with others. For example...the background shots at the very end, with Anaïs endeavoring to climb the plank, in the spirit of ascension, were actually underwater sand-banks seen from a plane I was traveling in over the Florida Keys, near Key West.

This brings me to say something about the use of superimposition in this film...as well as in almost all my other films... The initial idea of superimposition was suggested by Anaïs Nin herself, who said one day: "Why not project one film over another, and see what happens."

I tried to do this, and of course, for the most part it was a failure, because of phasing or slippage between the two films, but the momentary glimpses I had of what superimposition might be able to do gave me a feeling of ecstasy, especially in connection with this particular film with its emphasis on the submerged feelings and memories in all of us. I became convinced that superimposition in film corresponds to how we actually see, with two tier vision.

An example is "The Gondola Eye," a film I shot in Venice. I had placed myself in a gondola and in that special gliding motion one can only experience in a gondola, I shot every scene in the canals that my emotions responded to. When it came to editing the 12,000 feet I had shot over a three-year period ending in 1963, I found that since I had used my camera *only* when my emotions were aroused, I was in possession of an already emotionally charged thread, selected parts of which, when removed from their original context and juxtaposed or superimposed over different parts, would often reveal unexpected dimensions and new meanings.

I believe that this goes to the heart of filmmaking as a creative art...playing with images and sometimes the wonder of seeing reality transformed and the birth of a new reality.

Anyhow, it was with "Bells of Atlantis" that I vowed I would find the answer to the manifold technical problems involved in superimposition...

Actually, it was more than four years after the completion of "Bells of Atlantis," and thanks to the help of my friends Hilary Harris, Val Telberg, Alan de Forest, and Leo Lukianoff that we were able to construct an electro-mechanical apparatus, which I have used ever since, including the most recent film, "Luminescence," made in partnership with my friend the distinguished filmmaker, Arnold Eagle. The apparatus consists of two projectors held in sync by a magnetic field and a cine Kodak special camera in between, also in sync. All three focus on the same frame projected on the screen.

However...during the making of "Bells of Atlantis" I had the problem of how to do superimposition without the help of this apparatus. The solution at the time was what is called "sandwich printing" in the lab, literally printing one film on top of another. With the patient and devoted help of Ed Kasper, since deceased, but at that time the manager of what is now Filmtronics Labs, we succeeded in obtaining what I think were good results.

But it was a laborious, time-consuming, and expensive method. For example...when I had to use it in my next film, "Jazz of Lights," I wanted to make a 75 foot superimposed section. Just to make a selection of what was to go over what, I had to have two loops made of 1800 feet each. 3600 feet of printing altogether. Afterwards the selected combinations were sandwich printed.

Another collaborator for "Bells of Atlantis" who gave me invaluable help was my friend Len Lye, that incomparable filmmaker, who helped me to make some superimpositions in the camera which were used in the second part of the film, and also for a few feet at the beginning. But superimposing within the camera is a very risky method, since one mistake can destroy two films.

Anaïs Nin herself was my constant adviser, and it was a great satisfaction to me that she approved and valued the final work. She was particularly pleased when Abel Gance, who saw the film in Paris, proclaimed it "The first successful cinematic poem," and compared it to the experience he had in reading Rimbaud's "Le bateau ivre."

And I, of course, want to pay tribute to Louis and Bebe Barron, whose electronic sound track did so much to enhance the film. They had loved the poem for many years before I ever met them, and they were inspired to keep the background sound at a low level whenever the musical voice of Anaïs Nin was heard.

As for myself, I feel that with the technical problems involved in superimposition solved, I have been able to make a start in fulfilling my dream of being able to work on film in ways that are parallel to what I practiced for many years in painting and the graphic arts before I came to filmmaking.

*Hugh Guiler in New York*

I have often been asked: "Why did you abandon engraving and turn to filmmaking?" To answer this question I made a film entitled "Ian Hugo, Engraver & Filmmaker," in which I said, "I don't think I really abandoned the essentials. I just crossed a bridge and took with me the element of movement I had been trying to suggest in engraving." I then pointed out that in engraving I rarely made a drawing before plunging my graver into the plate, in the same way that in filmmaking I rarely made a script or even a screen treatment. In "Bells of Atlantis," and even in editing "Luminescence," my approach has always been to let a theme develop out of the material and not vice versa. In other words, not to impose an intellectual format to which the material had to conform. I feel that with this approach there is a better chance for the unconscious elements, which to me are the source of all inspiration, to emerge.

All this may sound pretty accidental and perhaps mysterious, but, as my engraving teacher S.W. Hayter used to say, "The happiest accidents seem to happen to the better artists."

It is also, I think true, that every artist worthy of the name has at some time penetrated beyond the known, and particularly beyond the intellectually known. The young generation today is fascinated by this mysterious area and many of them, for example, have been convinced that another of my films, "Melodic diversion," must have made under the influence of an "acid dip" [sic]. Not true. Nevertheless, when Feliciano Bejar, who made the glass and plastic sculptures in my film "Through the Magiscope," showed this film to the inmates of a prison in Denver, who were there because of crimes committed under the influence of drugs, these inmates asked to see the film three times because they said it was a better trip than any they had had.

This is perhaps one of the few cases where an artist is privileged to feel that he can be of some direct use to society.

I myself have been working on the frontiers of my dreams and have tried to liberate them from the cages of rigid forms, scripts and words. My aim has been to liberate the imagination by free association of meaningful images in such a way that each spectator can make his own associations and respond with his own feeling, as in music. It has in fact been remarked that my films are closer to music than to any of the other arts, except perhaps poetry. ◈

*Harry Kiakis*

## Memories of Reginald Pole

I met Reginald Pole in a roundabout way. In the late '50s, I belonged to an informal skin-diving club. In the summer months we would charter a boat, and dive near one of the channel islands, off the coast of southern California. We would spear fish, pry the plentiful abalone from rocks on the sea floor, then cook our catch on the beach, and drink lots of beer. We would sleep either on the boat, or on the beach.

It so happened that one of the divers, Scott George, was a young philosopher, given to thinking about the big questions: Why are we here? Where were we before birth? After death, are we reborn? And so he proposed that we meet once or twice a month to discuss these questions.

I found these meetings, attended by five or seven of us, to be very stimulating. At the time, some of those attending were reading the books of Gerald Heard, such as *Is God in History*, and *Pain, Sex and Time*. One evening, Walter Pennington had brought his friend, Reginald Pole. He was tall, dressed in a long black coat. Elderly, yet when he smiled, his unlined face appeared boyish. He spoke with a low, slow, mellifluous British accent. I had to wonder, who was this exotic bird that had landed in our midst? His comments were always apt and cogent, interspersed with quotations from Shakespeare.

After the meeting, a few of us, including Reginald, went to a coffee shop. We chatted about different subjects, and then one of us said, "Let's describe the book we are currently reading." When my turn came, I said "Oh, you wouldn't recognize the name of the author—Anaïs Nin." Reginald replied, very seriously, "She happens to be my daughter-in-law."

And so, as I got to know him, he would tell me the stories of a fascinating life. At Cambridge University, his classmates were Rupert Brooke and John Cowper Powys. He and Brooke belonged to the Marlow Society, where Reginald first knew his life was to be in the theatre. He often spoke of Cathleen Nesbitt, and her love of Rupert Brooke. How she went on to become a great actress.

At this stage of his life, Reginald was reduced to living in shabby "Residential Hotels," at the eastern end of Hollywood Boulevard, Sunset Boulevard, and small side streets. He moved often. Once, some of these hotels and apartment buildings must have been quite charming, with tropical foliage, Mexican tiles, and a fountain in the courtyard. Now, there was a half-dead, dusty palm tree, the fountain long gone dry, filled with cans and cigarette butts. To save on electricity, the halls and rooms were dimly lit. Reginald's room was in disorder, the night table covered with prescription drug bottles, as was the dresser. The room had a medicinal odor, partially offset by the eucalyptus smell in his various asthma inhalers. Other than his asthma, he appeared healthy enough, and I wondered why he needed all those drugs.

The most dramatic story of his life was when he fell in love with a Tahitian princess. He was a young man, and had gone to Tahiti after Rupert Brooke had told of his stay there, when Tahiti was still that Garden of Eden of the South Pacific. Word of his daughter's love for Reginald had gotten to the King. Soon, Reginald was warned that the King planned to have Reginald murdered. Late one night, Reginald swam out to a ship in the harbor, which was to leave early in the morning. For years Reginald and the princess corresponded. He showed me a stack of her letters. He gave me a conch shell from Tahiti, which I still have.

He would tell me of his visit to Robert Louis Stevenson's widow in Palm Springs, of his acting on the stage with John Barrymore. "When we had no dialogue, he would whisper to me, trying to get me to laugh."

He wrote a novel, based on his life, which was never published.

He disliked organ music. "Gloomy, funereal."

As if back on the stage, he often would enact his favorite Shakespeare passage, from *Measure for Measure*:

> ...but man, proud man
> Drest in a little brief authority,
> Most ignorant of what he's most assured,
> His glassy essence, like an angry ape,
> Plays such fantastic tricks before high heaven
> As make the angels weep...

One day, I introduced him to Connie, my wife-to-be. Both being romantics, the meeting went well. Reginald thought her Americanized name "Connie" did not suit her, and always addressed her by her Nicaraguan birth name, slowly pronouncing it, and pausing slightly between syllables "Con cep ción." As the days passed, Connie felt she had to do something about the condition of Reginald's room, so she packed a bag with cleaning supplies, took the bus, and cleaned the room. Upon return, she told me Reginald had lain in bed, murmuring, "Ah, Con cep ción, Angel of Mercy."

Reginald had a friend, Mary Evans, who would drive him to visit friends. When she was busy, I usually had time for the drive. Some visits stand out: his friend Eddie Kaminski, the photographer and teacher, lived in a small cottage, near UCLA. He worried how long it would be before his home was surrounded by high-rise office and apartment buildings. He described an experiment: he had friends do a simple step in the developing of a photo, but the resulting print revealed the distinctive character of each person.

Once, we went to a large Van Gogh exhibit, at the museum in Exposition Park.

At a reception in the Hollywood Hills two unusual incidents occurred. The house was designed by Neutra, who was there as a guest. The gathering was in honor of a German professor, who had taught for a few years at the University of Southern California, and was now returning to Germany. At one point, I found myself sitting on a sofa, with Lew Ayres on my right, and a tall, distinguished looking gentleman on my left. I had recently been told by a friend of a lunch he had with Henry Denison. They were both former monks-in-training in the Ramakrishna Order. My friend described their conversation, but gave me no description of Denison. On the sofa, a strong feeling overcame me, and I turned to my left and said, "Excuse me, but are you Henry Denison?" "Why yes, how did you know?"

Shortly afterwards, everyone in the room gasped—there had been a thud, and we saw the face of a young woman squashed up against the glass wall along one side of the living room.

Evidently, she had forgotten that the door was at the far end of the glass wall. She was shaken up, but not hurt physically.

Reginald would sometimes tell me of the marriage of Rupert and Anaïs: "Anaïs is in New York again. Her absences are very hard on my son." At that time, there were small theatres that showed foreign films. On some evenings, Connie and I would sometimes see Rupert leaving a theatre, looking very lonely.

I only once observed Reginald in a highly emotional state. I was walking towards his room, along one of those dim corridors, and saw Reginald up ahead, talking at the public phone that jutted from the wall. He was pleading: "Please! Please! Please!" I just stood there. His tall body was hanging on to the phone—I worried it would tear loose! When the conversation ended, I walked up to him, and nothing was said about his phone call.

One day, I received a call from Rupert. He and Anaïs were giving a birthday luncheon for Reginald, and we were invited, as the only guests. It was our first meeting with Rupert and Anaïs. They put us at ease; at one point Connie sat on my lap. Anaïs said how proud Rupert was of their new house. He had helped in the construction. Before moving in, they had lived in an apartment on Occidental Boulevard.

The newspapers had recently run articles about a group of astrologers in India, who were predicting the end of the world on February 17, 1962, the day of the luncheon. I made a lame joke: "I can't imagine better company to be in when the world ends."

Anaïs explained that all the furniture was Anne Baxter's; she had recently moved to Australia.

After a while, Connie and Anaïs spoke in Spanish. Anaïs seemed happy to be speaking a language she evidently did not get to use very often. She lost her composure only once that afternoon, when she said to Connie: "How *could* you go and clean that room!"

After a while, she asked Connie, "Would you like to see my dresses?" "Oh, yes!" Off they went, like two schoolgirls.

I talked with Anaïs about the drawbacks of fame. She described how once, at a reception, she had discovered a young woman crouched behind the sofa, listening to her conversation.

After lunch, Rupert brought out a tape recorder and a book of Keats' poems. "Dad, would you like to read for us?" We were all touched by the beauty of his voice. I wonder if that tape still exists.

As the years went by, Reginald grew weaker. I received a phone call from Mary Evans. Rupert had to place Reginald in a nursing home. And so I lost contact with Reginald. After a few years, Mary called to say that Reginald was stronger and would attend a gathering at her home. And so I went that evening, and there was Reginald, seated in a chair, his face still unlined. "Reginald, this is Harry, you remember him." He looked at me, trying to remember, and then he said, "Ah, Harry, I was crazy when I knew you!" ◈

*Paul Herron*

## Glimpses of Reginald Pole

*The dark side of the artist*

Beatrice Wood, in her memoir, recalls her introduction to Reginald Pole in 1923:

> Helen Freeman asked me to act in a play she'd written... She told me that a wonderful director was coming especially from California to help with the production. His name was Reginald Pole.
>
> He was a tall Englishman with a lean face and grey eyes full of twinkle. If his nose had been larger, he would have resembled Abraham Lincoln. His tweeds accentuated his bony structure and gave him an appealing male sharpness. He had been born in the Orient, where his parents were missionaries, and had gone to Christ College at Cambridge at the same time as Rupert Brooke, with whom he founded the Marlowe Society. Altogether charming and sophisticated, when his glance met mine I felt myself sigh like a cricket singing to the moon. (Wood 59)

By 1923, Pole had already lived a highly unconventional life, having had a dalliance with a Tahitian princess, having married and divorced Helen Taggart (with whom he had a son, Rupert, in 1919), and having been lured to California by the widow of Robert Louis Stevenson. His uncle, William Poel*, who was one of the world's most prominent Shakespeare producers, heavily influenced Pole's interest in the stage, where he rose to the point of performing with Boris Karloff, Estelle Winwood, and John Barrymore. Stark Young, who reviewed *Hamlet*, said of Pole's 1922 performance opposite Barrymore:

> Mr. Reginald Pole brought to the Ghost's lines a fine ear and an exact method of reading the verse that you gratefully detect before he is three lines under way. (Young 240)

In spite of Pole's apparent genius on the stage, he had begun showing signs of strange behavior. Wood describes how

> ...directors requested morning interviews with Reginald, but he declined, insisting that his asthma made it impossible for him to get up until noon. [But] I noticed that he caught morning trains when he

* *Apparently Poel's name was a misspelling which stuck.*

> wanted to. However, he truly was a "late night personality" and loved to roam the streets until two or three in the morning. I, who loathed both getting in bed too late and going for walks, went along with him as if I enjoyed it. My feminine philosophy dictated that a woman should do what a man wants. (Wood 62)

These peculiarities, which may seem minor on the surface, were hints of destructive forces that would thrust both him and those close to him into an abyss. Although Pole and Wood almost acted the part of a married couple, he would end up breaking her heart when he decided to marry an eighteen year old woman named Frances.

Nin, who met Reginald Pole in Denver on her famous cross-country trip with Rupert Pole in 1947, had first impressions that mirrored Wood's:

> He was an unusually handsome man, tall, very thin, with the long lean face of the Anglo-Saxon, pale-blue eyes under bushy eyebrows, refined features. My first impression of him was: this is the father I would like to have. (*Diary 5* 28)

It wasn't long before Nin began to note some of his disturbing traits:

> It seemed appropriate that Reginald should have acted the ghost in *Hamlet*. By the time I met him, I was seeing a ghost of himself. The underlying self-destruction which was corroding his marvelous gifts was already at work...
>
> His passion in the theater and literature did not rule his life. What ruled his life was an abnormal preoccupation with his body, his ambulant anxiety which made him move from one dismal hotel to another, sleep all day in darkened rooms, prowl at night when his friends were asleep and could not see him. (28)

When, in the late 1940s, Nin and Rupert Pole were together during her trips to California, Reginald began to come to visit them and stay until late at night, talking endlessly, trying "to fulfill an unfulfillable hunger, which was a return to passivity and a mother's care" (28).

Beatrice Wood also experienced these unannounced visits; Pole never completely exited her life, and came from time to time to replenish himself with her care.

> He occasionally spent time with us, sleeping on the couch in the sitting room, and although I firmly told him the room had to be

> presentable for visitors in the morning, he would sleep until noon. In addition, he did not make his bed. On top of this, he was a hypochondriac of the first order. We once counted nineteen bottles of medicine by his bed. He insisted night air was bad for him and nailed blankets to the windows to keep out air and light. In this closed atmosphere he burned foul smelling medicine. As a guest, Reginald was a disaster. (125)

One of Pole's friends, Ed Weinig, wrote Wood a letter his visit to Pole's hotel room:

> I saw Reginald Pole for about thirty minutes last Monday afternoon and wish to report to you.
>
> He smoked some kind of cigarette for emphysema and the odor...was almost unbearable for me. The windows were all tightly closed with bedspreads hanging over them. Food of days ago was scattered about the room and on the bed. Reginald was in bed, lower part pajamas, upper part shirt and tie awry.
>
> He told me all the "hard luck stories," including:
>
> 1. His doctor was out of town.
> 2. Rupert was vacationing somewhere in the South Seas.
> 3. He cannot write, except to sign his name.
> 4. Cannot walk more than a block or two.
> 5. Was confined to a sanitarium for two years, as a result of taking too many barbiturates...was released by a court, I believe he said.
>
> Then he turned to some kind of life after death, and strongly recommended that I read *The Betty Book* by Stewart Edward White. Reginald expected to meet us all after his and our death. (Wood 125)

Nin mentioned that he wore out his women, sucking them dry, going from one to the next, like his constantly changing hotel rooms. She wanted to say to him: "Reginald, come out of your darkened rooms. Come out in the light and the sun of day. Live with the friends who love you." But she felt his plea was: "Come and die with me. Keep me company in my death. Hold my hand while I lie in a state of non-existence" (*Diary 5* 29).

*Reginald with Rupert and Helen Taggart, 1920s*

As frank as Nin's published comments about Reginald are, they seem reserved compared to those in her original, handwritten diary of the time. We must remember that *Diary 5* was edited by Nin for publication some twenty years after it was written and a decade after Reginald's death, so her descriptions of him were perhaps mellowed by the passage of time and the relative ease of her life in 1974 compared to the early stages of her relationship with Rupert, when a sense of rhythm and certainty had not yet been established. The time they spent together often involved last minute arrangements after months of painful separation, complicated deceptions to keep Nin's husband Hugh Guiler from knowing where she had gone, and also to keep Rupert from discovering she had no intention of divorcing Guiler, although she had assured him she would. Nin lived in constant fear of being discovered, and there were many close calls—so the double life came at a very high price to her, and if she felt it was being was threatened, she became very insecure, and on many occasions she poured her misgivings and anger into the diary. To Nin, Reginald became an irritant, a thief who robbed her and Rupert of the precious time they had together.

December 7, 1950
TWA flight 34 en route for New York

The evening[s] [would have been] sweet if only Reginald [did] not appear, always unannounced in his dilapidated car. The physical resemblance between Reginald and Rupert is very startling. Rupert is a more sensuous and healthy edition... Reginald has an aristocratic air, but now he wears glasses and he does not have Rupert's full mouth. He is asthmatic, from the age of 5. He has all the neurotic symptoms that have been classified: masochism in food, obsession with his health...completely self-centered, he breathes with difficulty, gives himself insulin shots while he talks, monologues incessantly and plays a constant comedy of consulting us, asking for advice, confiding, planning, and then doing none of what is suggested. His activity is empty of meaning, direction or usefulness. He travels from one place to another in quest of relief. Now it is Riverside where he feels better near the desert. Endless monotonous, monotone discourses, free associations of dead impressions. His recollections of people are uninteresting because he has never known them or sees them clearly. They only exist in a tenuous relation to himself. Martha Graham was the women he trained to act in a play when she was a young girl student. Esther Winwood was a woman he once took a walk with and whom he did not kiss. Famous theatre directors were men who rejected or produced his version of *The Idiot*. Charles Chaplin is a man who invited him to dinner one night and asked him for auld lang zyne's sake to coach his son the reading of Shakespeare.

Reginald wrote a play about Lincoln because with little makeup, he can easily look like Lincoln, and he can act it so easily "because he has Lincoln's compassion." His taste in literature is arrested at his contemporaries' early stages of production. His responses are merely echoes of his Cambridge enthusiasm. The zombie quality of his speech is fatal. A death-ray, death radiations emanate from him. The static, stagnant atmosphere kills one's desire to give, help or talk because one knows it is a waste, a total waste. He will linger on, too long always, among the ashes he created in the evening, get in his car which, like himself, one wonders how it can reach the next place. He cannot be helped. He can only be served, washed, fed. He can only acquire an incubus parasite situation in the family he visits until people weary of his inordinate demands and escape from him. Now and then he arouses a protective instinct in a woman, he feeds on it until the woman feels the zombie at her breast and that no life will come of this, only a form of existence as repulsive as the fish without eyes, withered [fins], without propellers, who is less than a fish and only a little more than a stone, a static receiver of food who lies at the bottom of the aquarium.

At first I was devoted to Reginald out of an extension of my love for Rupert until his selfishness and madness frightened me, and I saw him for a human tick. Now I live merely in dread of his appearing when I have friends of my own there and he reads them his play on Lincoln for two hours. Rupert repairs his car, gives him money, clothes, but I have stopped trying to get his writings published or even to get him to fill out fellowship papers which he could do impressively due to his Cambridge academic proficiencies. His blindness to others is complete. He still goes to his former wife Helen for mail, for talks, while Lloyd* stands like a porcupine. For him I am a French writer who has too much sex in her work (as for Helen). But he likes my kindness to him, my warmth. (Unpublished diary)

In the early 1960s, after Reginald had recovered from a broken hip, Wood visited him in a rest home. As he, with the help of a nurse, feebly approached her, Wood said that in spite of his age and poor health that "he still held distinction." However, he deteriorated quickly, and near the end, he told Wood: "You are beautiful! I love your beautiful face...it has not changed much... I have done you wrong, I know that...but I have always loved you..." Then he said, "Sex is a funny thing, isn't it. It diverts...but my love for you has always been with me." Although she was sympathetic, she knew all of these utterances and his clinging sprang from his fear of dying alone (Wood 157).

Not long after, Wood received a letter from Anaïs Nin:

> Reginald has died in his sleep. Unconscious on Friday night. We went to see him, but he was gone. I am writing to you for Rupert. Reginald's ashes will be buried in England near his mother.
>
> To turn away from death, Rupert took me to your gallery, hoping your exhibit was still there, and it was... (Wood 157)

Wood replied:

> I weep and still weep, with you, and I rejoice that Reginald went in his sleep.
>
> I do not know why I weep—except that he allowed his body to go one way, his soul another. I weep that I could not do more to help him. Such a beloved person, so inwardly gentle—and so selfish. So wound within himself when it should have been otherwise.
>
> Years ago a very wise friend told me not to worry, that this life seemed to be one in which Reginald would just putter away, and that it was not his "fate" to accomplish his heart's dream. But I, like you, sensed his heights and wish he could have stayed there... You have been angelic to him. I hope now that he has slipped into another

---

* *Lloyd Wright, architect and son of Frank Lloyd Wright, who married Helen Taggart after her divorce from Reginald Pole.*

plane of existence, he fully realizes what you have been to him. (157-8)

While Reginald's death is not recorded in Nin's *Diary*, she acknowledges the many important friendships and professional associations that came from knowing him, including those with Aldous Huxley, Cornelia Runyon, and Alan Swallow, who would be the first American publisher to print all of her fiction. ◈

*Works Cited*

Nin, Anaïs. *The Diary of Anaïs Nin, Vol. 5, 1947-1955*. Ed. Gunther Stuhlmann. New York: Harcourt Brace Jovanovich, 1974.

Wood, Beatrice. *I Shock Myself: The Autobiography of Beatrice Wood.* San Francisco: Chronicle Books, 2006.

Young, Stark. "Hamlet." *Shakespeare in the Theatre: An Anthology of Criticism*. Ed. Stanley Wells. Oxford Press, 2000.

WORLD PREMIERE

of

"With Malice

Toward None"

by

REGINALD POLE

EMINENT BRITISH-AMERICAN ACTOR-PLAYWRIGHT

*With Mr. Pole in the role of*

Abraham Lincoln

*Sonya Blades*

## The Feminine Erotic

*Écriture féminine in Anaïs Nin's erotica*

*When I write, I feel I am more honest than when a man generalizes... Man's language is that displacement from the personal to the impersonal, but this is another form of self-deception. The self in them is disguised, it is not absent as they believe.*—Anaïs Nin, 1934

Decades before the modern French feminist movement, Anaïs Nin wrote in her diary of her conflicted feelings regarding sexual difference. She knew she must live in harmony with men in the patriarchal society she was subjected to, yet she could not help but feel a distinguishably feminine creative force within herself. Despite maintaining primarily male friendships and mentors, Nin struggled to assert her own rhythm and writing style, which, she felt, unfortunately could not be understood by her comrades. She lamented this feeling of isolation, wishing she could find someone with whom she could share her "world." She writes in her diary about her struggle: "Conflict between my feminine self who wants to live in a man-ruled world, to live in harmony with men, and the creator in me capable of creating a world of my own and a rhythm of my own which I can't find anyone to share" (*Diary 2* 62).

Ill-fatedly, Anaïs Nin died in 1977 from cancer, but if she had lived only a little longer, she might have found a comrade in France who had, just two years before Nin's death, published some of what is now considered part of the most influential writings on sexual difference. Hélène Cixous, a French feminist poet/philosopher/essayist, began writing in the 1970s on the relationship between sexuality and language, believing our sexuality is directly tied to how we communicate in society. The core "tenets" (Cixous would never use the term) appear in her essays entitled "The Laugh of the Medusa," "Sorties: Out and Out: Attacks/Ways Out/Forays," and "Castration or Decapitation?" Cixous denounces the strict disciplinarian nature of most theory, yet she creates an "idea" of l'écriture féminine—writing that is said to be feminine. I prefer the use of "idea" instead of the specific terminology of "theory" when referring to Cixous' work because she keeps her ideas abstract enough to lend themselves to various interpretations, and I will summarize my own interpretation of Cixous' body of work. Cixous avoids giving a solid definition, but she does give characteristics that may be attributed to a socially-constructed feminine writing.

Although Anaïs Nin claims she exemplifies a form of feminine writing in her erotica, many critics argue that Nin's descriptions of the erotic experience are merely a copy of the masculine pornographic conventions that objectify and oppress women through use of crude language and vulgar experiences. In contrast to these critics, I propose to analyze Anaïs Nin as writer of the feminine by applying Cixous' features of écriture féminine to Nin's erotic works, particularly the erotic short stories written in the 1940s that are now found in *Little Birds* and *Delta of Venus*. I believe Nin illustrates Cixous' expression of feminine writing and began the notion of écriture féminine before Cixous coined the term. I argue through her poetic portrayal of intimacy and sexual experience, through her diction, imagery, characterization, sentence structure, and plot sequences, Nin subverts, rather than copies, the male depiction of the erotic experience that has reinforced the objectification, domination, and oppression of women's sexuality. Nin prefigures Cixous' "theory" of écriture féminine to rewrite the erotic experience not only from a woman's experience and point of view, but in the writing style of "woman."

In order to find links between Nin's erotic short stories and Cixous' feminine writing, I must first venture a kind of definition and understanding of écriture féminine. The reason for "a kind of" definition is because Cixous feels a feminine practice is impossible to define, but I feel it is necessary to come up with an understanding and show how I interpret Cixous' "theory" because there have been many varying interpretations of écriture féminine. For Cixous, to define écriture féminine—to impose theory and coding—would be to reduce it to phallocentrism since "[écriture féminine] will be conceived of only by subjects who are breakers of automatisms, by peripheral figures that no authority can ever subjugate" ("Laugh of the Medusa" 883). Understanding that we live in a patriarchal society, Cixous allows for a pseudo-definition in her 1981 essay "Castration or Decapitation?" She describes a feminine textual body as a "female libidinal economy," endless with no closure and no origin, and no masculine question of "where do I come from?" because feminine writing starts on all sides at once. Instead, a feminine writing would prompt the question of giving: "What does this writing give? How does it give?" ("Castration" 53). This question of giving blends the roles of both reader and writer as a shared moment, giving authority to both since the writer gains authority through writing while also considering the impact of his or her voice on the reader.

Considering the idea of a shared moment of authority and voice, one important characteristic of écriture féminine is in fact a privilege of voice. Cixous argues that women have been denied their bodies, taught to ignore them through false sexual modesty, and made to feel that their own voices are incomprehensible as woman's voice because it "almost always falls on the deaf, masculine ear, which can only hear language that speaks in the masculine" ("Sorties" 92). Women engage in lyricism and singing of voice and must break the silence to leave the margin man has subjected her to, therefore giving her a sense of authority in her speaking. She is not easily understood by the masculine because her discourse is never simple or linear or "objectivized," universalized. She involves her story in history, therefore it is never ending and never follows a simple pattern. Similar to another French feminist known for her work concerning sexual difference, Luce Irigaray, Cixous states woman, being without "end," is also without principal "parts." Her libido is cosmic, overflowing, and has no fear of "going too far" as, in the Freudian sense, she has no fear of castration. As Irigaray would clarify in "This Sex Which Is Not One," the term placed on the idea of "woman" resists "adequate" definition, a patriarchal definition, because patriarchy will never understand her. According to Irigaray, our Western culture—an obviously patriarchal one—understands the concrete, the countable, the unit; however, "[woman] is neither one nor two" (Irigaray 26). Just as Cixous claims a cosmic, overflowing libido, Irigaray adds to the discussion "woman has sex organs more or less everywhere. She finds pleasure almost anywhere" (28). Masculine language may focus on the penis, but feminine writing has an endless feminine libidinal economy.

Irigaray further helps in an understanding of a feminine writing—or "womanspeak," as she would prefer—as she describes her views of writing the feminine. She understands the contradictions found in woman's writing "inaudible for whoever listens to them with ready-made grids" (29). She argues "one would have to listen with another ear, as if hearing an 'other meaning' always in the process of wearing itself, of embracing itself with words, but also of getting rid of words in order not to become fixed, congealed in them" (29). Irigaray enhances the argument of Cixous' feminine writing in "The Power of Discourse" as she describes the characteristics of feminine writing in almost the same words as Cixous: "its 'style' resists and explodes every firmly established form, figure, idea or concept...its 'style' cannot be upheld as a thesis, cannot be the object of a position" (79). Like Cixous, Irigaray also refutes a linear way of writing, stating it would no longer be possible if one were to employ woman's writing. Both Cixous and Irigaray portray the notion of nonlinear writing in their own works as each of their collections of essays blend together as one large work through common themes. In particular, reading one of Cixous' essays is akin to reading them all with a few minor elaborations in later works.

Unlike masculine writing which needs to know "how it runs" in order to "make it run" through a forced domination and manipulation, a writer employing écriture féminine feels free to play with sentences and structure while running away with syntax. She does away with personal pronouns and possessives for she is "in a pervasive relationship of desire with every being" ("Sorties" 96). The writer of écriture féminine refuses to accept the phallocentralized body, and it is her duty to relieve man of the phallus and to "return him to an erogenous field and libido that isn't stupidly organized round that monument, but appears shifting, diffused, taking on all the others of oneself" ("Castration" 51). Her writing is about multiplicity, and she "scrambles spatial order, disorienting it," moving things and values around, "emptying structures" and turning what is "proper upside down" ("Sorties" 96). In disrupting the patriarchal order she fights the urge to judge, diagnose, digest, and name—all laws of masculine writing. Cixous calls her feminine text "the text of the unforeseeable" ("Castration" 53) due to its detachment from the typical sequences found in masculine texts. It represents a metaphorical wandering, an excess that chances the incalculable and unknowable, making it appear disturbing and unpredictable to the masculine mind.

Cixous' main purpose for enacting écriture féminine is to promote societal change, to break down the patriarchy's hold on women's bodies. For Cixous, the only way we can escape this control is to break the silence and write through our bodies, creating our own language and discourse. Women must "invent the impregnable language that will wreck partitions, classes, and rhetorics, regulations and codes..." ("Laugh of the Medusa" 886). Cixous fosters her metaphor in "Sorties":

> Voice: unfastening, fracas. Fire! She shoots, she shoots away. Break. From their bodies where they have been buried, shut up and at the same time forbidden to take pleasure. Women have almost everything to write about femininity: about their sexuality, that is to say, about the infinite and mobile complexity of their becoming erotic, about the lightning ignitions of such a minuscule-vast region of their body... Woman's body with a thousand and one fiery hearths, when—shattering censorship and yokes—she lets it articulate the proliferation of meanings that runs through it in every direction. (94)

When woman writes of her libidinal economy, she seizes the moment to take control because of the enormity and variation of her libidinal drive; her imagination is "inexhaustible, like music, painting, writing: [her] stream of phantasms is incredible" ("Laugh" 876).

Cixous compares écriture féminine to a form of masturbatory writing, a "world of searching, the elaboration of a knowledge, on the basis of a systematic experimentation with the bodily functions, a passionate and precise interrogation of her erotogeneity ("Laugh" 876). She also uses the metaphor of women in flight so that women may leap forward in search of themselves and of their feminine sexual pleasure. Women must speak/write and affirm their difference. She must learn to speak of her pleasure, uncensoring her sexuality and "[tearing] her out of the superegoed, over-Mosesed structure where the same position of guilt is always reserved for her" ("Sorties" 97). She must explore her powers, her potency, and her strength. Only when women take up the pen and force their discourse into society's conversation can they break the shackles and free their never-ending voice/bodies: "Write yourself: your body must make itself heard. Then the huge resources of the unconscious will burst out. Finally the inexhaustible feminine Imaginary is going to be deployed. Without gold or black dollars, our naphtha will spread values over the world, unquoted values that will change the rules of the old game" ("Sorties" 97).

As opposed to the feminine libidinal economy, Cixous describes masculine sexuality and writing through notions of patriarchy such as obsession with power, control, and domination. In addition, it focuses on virility, authority, money, and man's own individual pleasure, "all of which reinforce his phallocentric narcissism" ("Sorties" 87). He enjoys his logic and his so-called truths. Typically, masculine writing either obscures women or reproduces the classic representations of women as sensitive, intuitive, and dreamy ("Laugh" 878), grossly exaggerating all the signs of sexual opposition, *not* sexual difference. Woman's body has been made the cause and location of inhibitions, with phallocentrism stealing her body and libidinal economy/drives. The masculine economy contains and takes away while the feminine never holds back and is always giving. It scorns hate—scorns the phallocentric concept of one master/one slave. Cixous views masculine writing as a repressive censorship of philosophical nomination/ conceptualization and urges the reader not to get trapped by names ("Castration" 52).

Cixous does not blame men as essentially patriarchal because patriarchy is beyond men as a social construction, and men suffer under the system as well because a society built upon dualistic power relations creates the idea that men must be dominant and competitive despite the real desires of each man as an individual. Cixous does admit that men have the ability to appropriate feminine writing, although they rarely do, which escapes the biological trap that often places men and women in essentialized roles while discrediting writing as a social construction. Cixous specifies that writings by women are not always feminine, and writings by men sometimes exhibit écriture féminine. Because of society, Cixous reasons, men have a difficult time breaking from law, moderation, and phallic authority due to the fact that "masculine profit is almost always mixed up with a success that is socially defined" ("Sorties" 87). Our Western culture puts value on the power and wealth of our men. On the other hand, women have the ability to transgress the power-play enforced on man, and they also have the advantage of what Cixous calls a "bisexuality." Due to her position in society, woman contains within herself the presence of both sexes. This bisexuality allows her to switch roles in accordance with her needs, also allowing her to understand both sides of the fence when it comes to writing. Although she may write either as man or woman, she must push past the urge to conform to a standard phallogocentrism. She must bring down the obsession with the phallus:

> Though masculine sexuality gravitates around the penis, engendering that centralized body (in political anatomy) under the dictatorship of its parts, woman does not bring about the same regionalization which serves the couple head/genitals and which is inscribed only within boundaries. Her libido is cosmic, just as her unconscious is worldwide. Her writing can only keep going, without ever inscribing or discerning contours, daring to make these vertiginous crossings of the other(s) ephemeral and passionate sojourns in him, her, them, whom she inhabits long enough to look at from the point closest to their unconscious from the movement they awaken, to love them at the point closest to their drives. ("Laugh" 889)

When supporting Anaïs Nin's appropriation of écriture féminine, and therefore disputing critics who argue that Nin supported masculine *pornographic* conventions, one must make a distinction between "erotica" and "pornography." While many would say there is no definite difference between the two—erotica is often referred to as "soft" porn that targets a female audience—Gloria Steinem disagrees in her pivotal essay entitled "Erotica and Pornography: A Clear and Present Difference." Steinem distinguishes the roots of the opposing terms, explaining how "erotica," from the root "eros," means "passionate love." This explanation is significant for two reasons: one, it gives the feeling of positive choice—of "free will, the yearning for a particular person" (37); secondly, the definition of erotica leaves open the question of gender. From the definition, one can assume that the subjects participating in a sexual act in erotica can fit into any number of combinations, including heterosexual, homosexual, and self-love. "Pornography," on the other hand, comes from the root "porno," meaning "prostitution" or "female captives," thus letting us know the subject is not mutual love, but domination and violence against women. Not only is the denotation negative, but it also supplies a gendered subject to be dominated: a female.

In "Pornography and Violence: What Does the New Research Say?" Diana Russell expounds on the differences between erotica and pornography. She describes pornography as "explicit representations of sexual behavior, verbal or pictorial, that have as a distinguishing characteristic the degrading or demeaning portrayal of human beings, especially women" (218). Although the idea is as negative as Steinem's depiction, she does include the possibility of the degradation of men. In contrast, "erotica" is "not degrading or demeaning women, men, or children" and it "often tends to be more subtle and/or artistic than is usual for sexually explicit materials" (219). Russell's description provides more information concerning the style and structure of erotica, as well as content, whether a movie or in written literature.

If pornography is comparable to a masculine sexual writing, then we can assume that masculine sexual writing/pornographic convention supports the patriarchal, phallocentric subjugation of women as it portrays dominance, the use of the "other's" body, humiliation, and violence. Like Cixous' description of masculine writing, pornography uses the sexual experience to display power and control, using sex as a weapon. Therefore, if Anaïs Nin appropriates a feminine writing, her writing would defy pornographic convention and focus more on shared pleasure, sensuality, and mutual respect in addition to the other characteristics of écriture féminine described earlier. Furthermore, Nin would have to play with and rework sexual imagery through, for example, role-reversal—depicting men as passive and objectified—in order to break down the generic definitions associated with gendered sexuality. While this may repeat the objectification of pornography, one could view this role reversal as a mimetic device that shows the complication of simplified gender identification, which could in turn challenge previous depictions of woman as object.

Before providing examples of Nin's feminine writing, I would like to contrast her writing to that of her mentor and "friend," Henry Miller. I use the term "friend" loosely because although they shared a sexual and artistic relationship, Nin and Miller's relationship became complicated as Nin began to write in her own style. Furthermore, Miller was often cruel to Nin, using her for her money, stealing her ideas for his own works, and scornfully mocking her poetry in parodic episodes in his own stories. Lynette Felber argues in "Mentors,

Protégés, and Lovers" that Nin's relationship with Miller created a kind of productive antagonism as Nin began to rebel against her lover's conception of art while finding her own identity as a writer, and "this configuration is likely to produce tension, infusing both the mutual professional interest and the romance" (167). Felber argues that since Miller was twelve years Nin's senior, as well as being more experienced and confident in his writing ability, the relationship between the two began as a classic mentorship; however, Nin quickly assumed the role of patron, "thus it was Nin who offered Miller protection and a kind of sponsorship, the usual function of the mentor rather than the protégé" (170). Perhaps Miller saw a talent in Nin that differed positively from his own style because shortly after Nin showed Miller her written description of his wife June, "Miller 'stole' her observations to use in his own depictions of his wife in *Tropic of Capricorn*" (Felber 177). When Nin discovered Miller's deception, she wrote in her diary:

> I discovered that I had given away to Henry all my insights into June, and that he is using them. He has taken all my sketches for her portrait. I feel empty-handed, and he knows it, because he writes me that he "feels like a crook." And what have I left to work with? He is deepening his portrait with all the truths I have given him. What was left for me to do? (*Diary 1* 128)

Nin answers her own question using ideas similar to Cixous' écriture féminine. Her answer is "To go where Henry cannot go, into the Myth, into June's dreams, fantasies, into the poetry of June. To write as a woman, and as a woman only" (128). Miller may have taken the outward "truths" of Nin's depiction, but Nin shows that he cannot understand, and therefore cannot use, the art of woman's writing to show June's *inner* being.

Unlike Nin, the works of Henry Miller illustrate the masculine pornographic convention, particularly his core work *Tropic of Cancer.* In his slightly autobiographical/fictional travelogue, Miller only refers to women sexually, and usually with misogynistic overtones. He continuously calls the women throughout the book "cunts," "bitches," and "whores" while describing vulgar, disgusting, and humiliating sex acts. In addition, Miller describes women as giant sex organs (or "pussies" or "twats" as he would prefer), particularly when referring to the prostitutes who repeatedly appear throughout the novel. The terminology Miller uses conveys an image of women as objects, focusing on the lowliest slang terms imaginable for the female body. An example:

O Tania, where now is that warm cunt of yours, those fat, heavy garters, those soft, bulging thighs? There is a bone in my prick six inches long. I will ream out every wrinkle in your cunt, Tania, big with seed. I will send you home to your Sylvester with an ache in your belly and your womb turned inside out. Your Sylvester! Yes, he knows how to build a fire, but I know how to inflame a cunt. I shoot hot bolts into you, Tania, I make your ovaries incandescent. Your Sylvester is a little jealous now? He feels something, does he? He feels the remnants of my big prick. I have set the shores a little wider... After me you can take on stallions, bulls, rams, drakes, St. Bernards. You can stuff toads, bats, lizards up your rectum. You can shit arpeggios if you like... I am fucking you, Tania, so that you'll stay fucked... (*Tropic of Cancer* 5-6).

Not only are the words base and the images almost clinical in description, Miller also demonstrates the "divide and conquer" mentality of both women and the men with whom he competes. He insists that once he has "had" the female she will forever be marked by his "enormous member," an example of pornographic crudity, the oppression of women, and the penis-obsessed/phallocentric notions of masculine language.

Lynette Felber observes the distinctions between Miller's and Nin's sexual language, advocating a difference in both point of view and style. She asserts the explicitness of Nin's writing; however, Felber claims that Nin utilizes sensual and extravagant surrealist images, while Miller uses an absurdist language that can be *too* real with a Rabelaisian vulgarity as it "depicts women from a perspective of limited 'insight' that can only be called masculinist, in the most pejorative sense of the word" (Felber 174). Anaïs Nin was not blind to the differences between her own writing and that of Henry Miller. Nin writes in her diary "I get so tired of his obscenities, of his world of 'shit, cunt, prick, bastard, crotch, bitch'" (*Diary 1* 55). Nin adds, "At moments he can say the most delicate and profound things. But this gentleness is treacherous because when he sits down to write, he denies this; he does not write with love but with anger, he writes to attack, to ridicule, to destroy. He is always against something. Anger incites him; fuels him" (55). She stresses her difference from Miller: "Anger poisons me" (55). She will later assert in her diary that "the key to Henry's work is contained in the word burlesque. What he writes is a burlesque of sex, a burlesque of ideas...a burlesque of life" (*Diary 2* 62). Nin concludes, "What I feel is too deep and too human for that" (62). When first writing her erotic short fiction, Nin realized she and other writers of erotic literature had only one model—the writing of men (*Delta of Venus* xii). Like Cixous, Nin felt women must affirm their differences in writing, championing the feminine over a form of androgyny (Felber 168). In her essay, Felber reasons that Nin's intention was to develop a language of her own, one that would surpass the style of her own mentors, including Miller, who could never understand her way of writing. She argues that Nin purposefully chose to cultivate a "feminine" identity, reaching for her own autonomy (177). Like Cixous, Anaïs Nin claims that her reason for appropriating a distinctively feminine writing is to promote change, or autonomy, to help women free themselves—to soar through the air, as Cixous would later describe it.

Anaïs Nin and Hélène Cixous share more than a love of poetic, feminine writing. They both were unsure of their writing abilities, worrying how others would perceive their works. Cixous feared her own strengths and drives, fearing her own desire to write her own way. She writes: "You are mad! What's the meaning of these waves, these floods, these outbursts?" ("Laugh" 876). By the time Cixous wrote "The Laugh of the Medusa," she understood how women are made to believe that they are well adjusted only if they have "divine composure." Nin felt the same pressure from society, enough so that she buried her own work, hiding the erotic stories she had written for money during her days of "literary prostitution." Years later Anaïs Nin would look back at those stories, rereading them only to find that her own voice had not been completely suppressed: "In numerous passages I was intuitively using a woman's language, seeing sexual experience from a woman's point of view" (*Delta of Venus* xvi).*

Secondly, both women assign themselves to a study of the unconscious, perhaps due to similar childhood situations. They both were raised in culturally mixed households: Cixous' mother had Austro-German ancestry, and her father had French-colonial and Jewish origins; Nin's mother was a Cuban of French-Danish descent, and her father was Spanish-Cuban. Cixous felt she did not belong, straddling the borders of two very different worlds (Bray 2). Although Nin did not feel exclusion, she did move between France and America several times during her life, making it difficult to adjust to any one concept of cultural identity. In addition, like Cixous, Nin lost her father at a young age; however, unlike Cixous, it was not from death. Nin's father left her and her mother when Nin was a child, fostering in her a sense of loss and betrayal. Shortly after referring to her father's

---

* *John Ferrone, editor of Nin's erotica, is not convinced that Nin really believed this. See* A Café in Space, *Vol. 7, p. 57.—Ed.*

coldness in her diary, Nin writes, "I always thought that one had to *deserve* love, I worked so hard to merit it" (*Diary 1* 176). Cixous and Nin would continue to carry this emotional baggage throughout their lives, trying to compensate for this first loss through an understanding of writing.

Through this fascination with the unconscious and hidden drives, Anaïs Nin created her own ideas pertaining to a feminine writing. Similar to Cixous' écriture féminine, Nin created works connecting the story and the dream—"the flow and absence of rational pattern" (Hoy 65). Nin wrote in her diaries for over thirty years trying to understand her own unconscious, and she developed her works around these diary entries with the goal of destroying the barriers between the conscious and unconscious, "the elimination of the artificial divisions of time into past, present and future, so that experience occurred in some inner space where everything was simultaneously accessible to the conscious mind," creating a world "without end—a cosmic vision" (Hoy 65). Nin's unconscious parallels Cixous' écriture féminine in that both are timeless, flowing, and "cosmic." Nin's diaries are the greatest example of this timeless endlessness as she draws on stories and references from various moments in her life.

Furthermore, Nin may be understood as Cixous' comrade in controversy. Critics of both Cixous and Nin maintain they promote essentialism due to their distinctions between masculine and feminine, as though these characteristics are innately part of one's physical sex. Cixous defends herself by saying that anatomical sex or essence is not what determines who we are. On the contrary, she argues that history and culture all play a part in who we have become. Therefore, the stress on sexual difference is "an effect of representation and, as such, capable of being subverted and remade" (Bray 21). The fact that masculine and feminine writings are not tied to biologically sexed bodies is apparent because men can write écriture féminine, and vice versa. Cixous actually uses feminine writing as a metaphor for expanding discourse to include different ways of writing or speaking in a less totalitarian way than what is usually accepted as a standard (and often academic) form of communication. Abigail Bray furthers Cixous' argument, stating that "we must develop autonomous definitions of woman and femininity for it is only then that the phallocentric dialectic of man/not-man, self/other can be challenged" (21), showing how an assertion of sexual difference promotes societal change. Nin parallels Cixous in "Eroticism in Women," adding that we must "peel off the false selves, the programmed selves, the selves created by our families, our culture, our religions" (4). By doing so, people can undermine the sexuality centered around control and power that has been built by patriarchy, but the only way it can be accomplished is for men to find the femininity in themselves and for women to accept the masculinity in themselves—a form of Cixousian bisexuality. Like Nin, Cixous acknowledges the ineffectiveness of gender neutrality because neutrality is artistically limiting and falls prey to both an exclusionary majority and divisions in difference. In opposition to gender neutrality, Cixous lauds bisexuality beyond Irigaray's survivalism and inevitable social construction: bisexuality becomes the solution for a multiplicity of desire ("Sorties" 84-85).

In addition to the controversy surrounding issues of essentialism, Anaïs Nin and Hélène Cixous have both been accused of unrealistic, petty bourgeois writing that takes no political responsibility. For example, in an article in *The New Yorker* entitled "Sex, Lies, and Thirty-Five Thousand Pages," Claudia Pierpont criticizes Nin as both a pseudo-artist and a self-made character (rather than a "real" human being), including her "immoral" lifestyle as a sex-addicted polygamist, arguing that Nin was a narcissistic liar. Pierpont suggests that when Nin found Surrealism in Paris, the "'modern spirit' became an excuse for unintelligible writing, as her father's desertion was the excuse for her games of betrayal" (Pierpont 77). She mentions that Nin's friends would read her works and beg her to give them more concrete, pictorial writing (77). The article ends in judgment of Nin's dishonesty about her abortion. Pierpont references Nin's short story entitled "Birth," which Pierpont implies is a distortion and a lie concerning Nin's experience of pregnancy. While the story "Birth" describes a miscarriage, Pierpont asserts that Nin's diary explicitly tells of Nin's desire to rid herself of her problematic pregnancy through abortion while Nin purposefully portrays herself as a martyr to her art (89). Pierpont declares, "This is a horrifying scene, if not in the way that Nin intended, and is perhaps, even now, a dangerous one" (90). Pierpont is referring to the idea that Nin's dismissal of her abortion could have had serious political implications. While Pierpont valorizes women who are open to the public about having an abortion, she states of Nin's case: "In this instance, rewriting her history was probably Nin's best deed for the feminist cause, and her most important lie" (90) because of what Pierpont views as a self-inverted and self-important flaw on the part of Nin. For Pierpont, Nin's embellishments and "obscene" lifestyle come together to create a woman who deserved nothing but pity and who had nothing positive to offer society.

In *Sexual/Textual Politics*, Toril Moi criticizes Cixous, arguing that there is a libertarian individualism running through her work that fails to take into account the complex political realities women face. She describes an incident when Cixous wore an ermine coat to one of her lectures. Moi writes, "Ermine as emancipation: it is odd that the women of the Third World have been so ludicrously slow to take up Cixous' sartorial strategy" (Moi 126). Viewing Cixous' essays as overly utopian, Moi feels Cixous' wearing an ermine coat shows her lack of political consciousness, a self-interested aestheticism, an indulgent sensuality, and a failure to provide useful strategies for forming feminist identities. However, like Nin, Cixous blatantly declared her ambivalence toward politics and never declared herself a feminist. In an interview in 1976, Cixous goes so far as to suggest a link between politics and patriarchy when she states that masculine structures have "a tendency to edification, to centralization (which inserts itself within a political reality under the guise of state, of leader, of nation), which goes back to the father, back to the mind, back to government..." ("Rethinking Differences" 74). Like Nin, Cixous would describe some forms of feminism as patriarchal—some only want to copy what has already been done to them by a patriarchal system—or, as Nin would say, some women are just trying to be like men. Both women would rather change the system than fight to become the system.

The critics have attacked not only Nin's character and ideas, but also her literary works as well. In a book review for Nin's *Delta of Venus*, Albert Carter argues that Nin concentrates solely on sex and creates a predictable variation of erotica centered on voyeurism, anonymous lovemaking, fetishism, and exhibitionism. He states, "In leaving out the poetry, the stories are weak in characterization, plot, and over-all themes," and he argues that the stories are written in the male tradition (Carter 409). Bruce Bawer, a critic for *The New York Times*, agrees with Carter, adding: "If Nin is remembered at all, it will not be as a pioneer but as a colorful peripheral character who embodied...some of the more unfortunate distinguishing characteristics of our age...a rejection of intellect in favor of feeling...selfishness and irresponsibility" (Bawer 10). In response to these remarks, Cixous would claim these two *men*, the masculinist writers that they are, cannot understand Anaïs Nin's feminine writing. The features these men denounce—weakness of plot, weakness of themes, and rejection of intellect—are a few of the characteristics Cixous hails as écriture féminine. Just as important is the way that these critics distort what is actually in Nin's stories. Anaïs Nin does not focus only on sex, and her writing does not focus on masculine convention and predictability.

For example, one of the shorter stories in Nin's *Delta of Venus*, "Mallorca," contains no concrete descriptions of sexual intercourse whatsoever. The story begins with "I was spending the summer in Mallorca" (34), giving the feel of only part of a story, like a chapter from a book. It appears continuous and infinite, with no beginning or end. Then, in the next paragraph, the narrator says, "one evening some years go," adding to a sense of timelessness. Concrete time is of no concern to Nin's narrator. The narrator includes lyrical language with water imagery, one of Cixous' recurring images of the feminine libidinal economy: "Walking thus and dreaming and watching the effects of the moon on the sea, the soft lapping of the waves at her feet..." (35). Nin's description compares to Cixous' imagery: "I, too, overflow; my desires have invented new desires, my body knows unheard-of songs" ("Laugh" 876)—a bursting forth and overflow of fluidity.

In the story, a fisherman's daughter walks along the shore one moonlit evening and comes across someone swimming nude by the cove, someone who she believes is an American woman she had met the day before. The girl is in a dream-like trance and is so enthralled by her natural surroundings, "the effects of the moon on the sea, the soft lapping of the waves at her feet," that she does not question the sex of the person she can barely see (35). When the person calls to her, the fisherman's daughter uses gender-unspecific language by referring to "the voice." All she can see are unidentifiable, and therefore unsexed, body parts such as the bobbing of a head and the movement of an arm in the water, which coincides with Cixous' focus on endlessness and a lack of origin because both the fisherman's daughter and the reader have no closure as to where the parts begin or end. The girl soon realizes the person is actually the American woman's younger brother who then seduces her and "[takes] her there in the water, swaying floating...the wavelike movements of their bodies as they enjoyed each other seemed part of the sea...they found a foothold on a rock and stood together, caressed by the waves, and shaking from the orgasm" (37). The girl repeatedly refers to the boy/man (this is also not made specific) as "her friend," and refers to his body as "her friend's body" (36). Her sexual identity is ambiguous because she had been aroused without knowing the sex of the person swimming, then had been sexually intrigued believing "her friend" to be female, and then when she does realize "her friend" is male, she maintains her arousal. Apparently the sex and any other particulars are unimportant to the fisherman's daughter. Nin's language and sexual imagery differ from the previously quoted passage from Henry Miller because there is no vulgarity, no objectification, and it is written in a beautifully lyrical and metaphorical language. Rabelais would have been greatly disappointed.

The story ends with the narrator's reminiscences as she still feels she can see them swimming together and making love. The story is simple, yet beautifully written; and Nin, as in Cixous' écriture féminine, does not try to infuse it with logic nor closure, for there is nothing to figure out. It is simple, with no judgments to be made—a spontaneous, natural overflowing; a "writing of the womb," as Nin would say. And in support of Cixous' écriture féminine and writing the body, Nin could never be said to be a victim of "false sexual modesty." Many of Nin's erotic short stories come from passages in her diaries and from friends' experiences, adding to a paradoxically nonlinear continuity because experiential segments blend into a holistic "knowledge" or "life." In addition, several characters, including the character named Manuel, appear in different stories as though their narratives overlap into others' accounts.

Speaking of "Manuel," the story itself turns convention upside down. In the preface to *Delta of Venus,* Nin describes how she would write erotica for a dollar a page. The collector of her erotica would always tell her to leave out the poetry and concentrate only on sex, so Nin began to write tongue-in-cheek, "to become outlandish, inventive, and so exaggerated that I thought he would realize I was caricaturing sexuality. But there was no protest" (*Delta* ix). "Manuel" is humorous in its depictions, showing the ridiculousness of masculine sexual conventions. Nin not only reverses the role of the objectified by making the man the object to be gazed upon, but she does so in an exaggerated manner to make the man appear foolish for his penis obsession. Manuel agrees to do a woman's housework if she will look adoringly at his penis. The woman dramatically praises Manuel's penis, and as she does so he becomes so excited that he collapses to the floor and ejaculates onto his own face (257).

Another example of parodic role-reversal is found in the erotic short story "The Veiled Woman." While the story appears to be about a nymphomaniac who finds random men in bars to "use" her for their own sexual pleasure, the reader cannot help but notice the recurring image of the mirror and how the woman cannot become aroused until she sees their actions reflected back to her. The "veiled woman," who had been so attractive in her mysteriousness, becomes the voyeur in her own fantasy, and the man who had thought himself the "colonizer" who "loved to recount his exploits...hint[ing] that as soon as he set foot in the street some adventure presented itself, that he was never at a loss for an interesting evening, or for an interesting woman," becomes the object to be gazed upon (88). Eventually the man will discover that he has not only been the object of the woman's gaze when a friend, "a confirmed voyeur," tells him a story of when he had witnessed a passionate episode between a man and a woman in a mysterious house filled with mirrors. The "adventurous" man realizes that he has been made a spectacle for the entertainment of others, and he leaves both embarrassed and enlightened to the "playacting" often used between men and woman (96).

As a last example of Nin's portrayal of écriture féminine, "The Woman on the Dunes" addresses concepts of a more positive role-reversal, intimacy, and Cixous' idea of mutually shared sexual experience. The main character, a man named Louis, is sexually aroused and decides to wander aimlessly to appease his fever. From the beginning Nin shows her use of bisexuality, trying to understand the story through the experiences and sexuality of a man. Also, Nin includes water imagery yet again as she describes the sounds of the ocean's "rhythmic movements" (*Little Birds* 23). Louis sees a woman remove her clothing and run into the waves, so he follows in pursuit. Although strangers, both are mutually caught up in the thrill and begin to tease each other playfully. Their passions reaching new heights, the couple run onto the beach, laughing and dripping with water; however, when trying to make love to the woman, Louis repeatedly loses his erection. He is humiliated, but the woman consoles him saying there is plenty of time, and then a role-reversal takes place. The woman demands Louis stick out his tongue while they kiss, the narrator describing "she let him, now and then, touch his tongue against hers. She let him pant like a dog in heat, open his being, stretch towards her" (25). The woman has become the aggressor, placing demands and allowing Louis sexual pleasure on her behalf.

After making love the woman tells Louis a story about a woman who had made love to someone she had never seen. She describes the scene without use of possession of body parts, giving the feeling of shared disconnectedness:

> She felt dizzy with conflicting sensations. She did not move or turn her head. A hand now sought an opening in the skirt and discovered the buttons. Each button undone by the hand made her grasp with both fear and relief. The hand waited to see if she protested before proceeding to another button. She did not move (28).

Nin uses a vagueness of sexuality and gender as "the hand" is never possessed by an individual, nor is it sexed. Nin describes another scene of disconnected frenzy and random, unpossessed, and unsexed parts in her erotic short story "Marianne," who recalls penny movies she had once seen in Paris:

> ...of figures rolling on the grass, hands fumbling, white pants being opened by eager hands, caresses, caresses, and pleasure making the bodies curl and undulate, pleasure running over their skins like water,

causing them to undulate as the wave of pleasure caught their bellies or hips, or as it ran up their spine or down their legs (*Delta* 81).

There is a "rhythmic and unusual irregularity" when Nin describes sensuality or sexuality (Papachristou 59), and she uses commas and repetition as a sense of urgency and built-up desire. Again, in the above quote, the reader does not know who is doing each action nor to whom the random body parts belong. Papachristou explains in Nin's erotic writing, "an abstract definition corresponds to every concrete movement," making "lived sensations and feelings concrete, to preserve them with words that create images" (60). Nin uses tangibility to convey her abstract ideas and the unconscious in a way that resembles the imagery Cixous uses throughout her essays, particularly when Cixous uses the image of a laughing Medusa to show the different meanings it conveys depending on one's sex.

The story "Marianne" contributes to écriture féminine through its use of sexual ambiguity and the writing of the body. This layered story begins with a sort-of autobiographical first-person narration when Nin refers to an "I" who calls herself "the madam of a house of literary prostitution," which is a direct reference to Nin's own career as an erotic writer (*Delta* 74). The narrator hires a young painter named Marianne to type her erotic stories—a woman who had previously had many unfulfilling sexual experiences. The narrator hopes, as Nin possibly hopes, that the reading of the erotic fiction will awaken something sensual within Marianne. Marianne becomes affected enough to be "taken with the desire to write down her own experiences" and reflect on the past (76). She begins by admitting that "most of what happened to [her] was clinical, anatomical. Here were the sexes touching, mingling, but without any sparks, wildness, sensation" (76). She asks herself, "How can I attain this? How can I begin to *feel*—to *feel*?" (76). This description brings to mind the problems with Miller's writing style when he demonstrates the vulgarity of the purely physical and "clinical." Nin asserts that in order to feel true eroticism, one must move beyond the physical into feeling and emotion. The reader is soon introduced to Fred, a man who, similar to the man in "Manuel," can only become aroused if he has been made the object; however, Fred differs from Manuel because his need for adoration is not made ridiculous. In contrast, Fred has a kind of innocence and sexual ambiguity in his embarrassment over his fetish. He stutters his request to become the painter's model, and he blushes "like a woman" (76). Since Fred's story is being told by a woman, we get no description of her physicality. We only hear of how she "studied his violet eyes, the fine, gold, downy hair on his hands, the fine hair on the top of his ears" (77). Fred becomes the object of desire, and interestingly that object has "a faunish air and a feminine evasiveness which attracted [her]" (77). There is ambiguity in who is the object and who is the subject, and there is also sexual ambiguity concerning masculine and feminine roles and concerning the sexual preference of a speaker who sleeps with men but is highly attracted to this seemingly effeminate man.

The collector's insistence that Anaïs Nin leave out the poetry and concentrate only on sex inspired her to come to a greater understanding of what it means to write "woman," what she would contribute as a form of poetry, or a deeper understanding of the unconscious and hidden drives. Although not as apparent as in her longer fiction, Nin holds to her feminine writing in her erotic short fiction, finding that she cannot leave out the poetry as the collector had insisted. To leave out the poetry would be to leave out the sexual experience, for who wants to read a clinical description of a penis inserted in a vagina? As to Cixous' question of "what does this text give?" and "how does this text give?", Nin would answer: "It gives sexual pleasure or jouissance. How? Through the writings of woman." ◈

*Works Cited*


Bawer, Bruce. "I Gave So Much to Others?" *The New York Times.* 5 March, 1995: 10.

Bray, Abigail. *Hélène Cixous: Writing and Sexual Difference.* New York: Palgrave Macmillan, 2004.

Cixous, Hélène. "Castration or Decapitation?" *Signs.* 7.1. (Autumn, 1981): 41-55.

----. "The Laugh of the Medusa." *Signs.* 1.4 (Summer, 1976): 875-893.

----. "Rethinking Differences: An Interview." *Homosexualities and French Literature.* Ed. George Stambolian and Elaine Marks. New York: Cornell University Press, 1979: 70-86.

----. "Sorties." *The Newly Born Woman.* Minneapolis: University of Minnesota Press, 1975: 63-132.

Felber, Lynette. "Mentors, Protégés, and Lovers: Literary Liaisons and Mentorship Dialogues in Anaïs Nin's 'Diary' and Dorothy Richardson's 'Pilgrimage.'" *Frontiers: A Journal of Women Studies.* 15.3. (1995): 167-185.

Howard Carter, Albert. "Anaïs Nin: *Delta of Venus*: Erotica" (Book Review). *Studies In Short Fiction.* 14.4 (Fall 1977): 409-410.

Hoy, Nancy Jo. "The Poetry of Experience." *Anaïs: An International Journal, Vol. 4.* Ed. Gunther Stuhlmann. Becket, MA: Anaïs Nin Foundation, 1986: 52-66.

Irigaray, Luce. *This Sex Which is Not One.* New York: Cornell University Press, 1985.

Miller, Henry. *Tropic of Cancer.* New York: Grove Press, 1961.

Moi, Toril. *Sexual/Textual Politics.* New York: Methuen, 1985.

Nin, Anaïs. *Delta of Venus.* New York: Pocket Books, 1977.

----. *The Diary of Anaïs Nin*, Volume 1. Ed. Gunther Stuhlmann. New York: The Swallow Press/Harcourt Brace Jovanovich, 1966.

----. *The Diary of Anaïs Nin*, Volume 2. Ed. Gunther Stuhlmann. New York: The Swallow Press/Harcourt Brace & World, 1967.

----. "Eroticism in Women." *In Favor of the Sensitive Man and Other Essays.* New York: Harvest Books, 1966: 3-11.

----. *Little Birds.* New York: Pocket Books, 1979.

Papachristou, Sophia. "The Body in the Diary." *Anaïs: An International Journal, Vol. 9.* Ed. Gunther Stuhlmann. Becket, MA: Anaïs Nin Foundation, 1991: 58-66.

Pierpont, Claudia Roth. "Sex, Lies, and Thirty-five Thousand Pages." *The New Yorker.* 69 (March 1993): 4-90.

Russell, Diana E.H. "Pornography and Violence: What Does the New Research Say?" *Take Back the Night.* New York: William Morrow and Company, 1980: 218-238.

Steinem, Gloria. "Erotica and Pornography: A Clear and Present Difference." *Take Back The Night.* New York: William Morrow and Company, 1980: 35-39.

*Anita Jarczok*

## Eroticizing Nin, Eroticizing Women

*Philip Kaufman's* Henry & June

The movie *Henry & June* was made by a well-known director, distributed by a major studio, and starring then recognizable and now famous actors. Directed by Phillip Kaufman and distributed by Universal Pictures, it starred Maria de Medeiros as Anaïs Nin, Uma Thurman as June Miller, Fred Ward as Henry Miller, Richard E. Grant as Hugh Guiler, and Kevin Spacey as Richard Osborn, Miller's friend. Released in 1990, *Henry & June* earned $1,032,492 during its first weekend of release, and $11,567,449 in total (IMDb The Internet Movie Database), which is a respectable sum of money, especially for an NC-17 rated film. As Jody Pennington notes, *Henry & June* and *Showgirls* (1995) were the only NC-17 rated movies that grossed over ten million dollars (Pennington 91).

Before Kaufman undertook the *Henry & June* project, he had already adapted and directed *The Right Stuff* (1983), based on Tom Wolfe's book, and *The Unbearable Lightness of Being* (1988), based on Milan Kundera's novel. Both movies were considerably successful. *The Right Stuff* was nominated for eight Academy Awards, including Best Picture, and won four of them (Best Effects, Best Film Editing, Best Music, Best Sound). *The Unbearable Lightness of Being* was nominated for two Oscars, one for cinematography and the other for adapted screenplay. Therefore, Kaufman began *Henry & June* with very good credentials.

As for the cast, Kaufman managed to bring together a group of budding actors. Uma Thurman had appeared in a few movies before *Henry & June*, including *Dangerous Liaisons* (1988), but her career really blossomed after 1990. Since then, she has starred in a variety of films, ranging from romantic comedies to action movies, but she is probably best remembered for her roles in Quentin Tarantino's *Pulp Fiction* (1994) and *Kill Bill* vols. I and II (2003; 2004). In *Henry & June* she stars as sensual and unpredictable June Miller. Maria de Medeiros, who plays Anaïs Nin, is a Portuguese born actress who has been in both European and American productions, and who, as reviewers of *Henry & June* stated repeatedly, bears a striking resemblance to the character she plays. Fred Ward, who collaborated earlier with Kaufman on *The Right Stuff*, portrays Henry Miller. Richard E. Grant, whose career was launched in a cult British black comedy *Whitnail and I* (1987), appears here as Nin's devoted husband Hugh (Hugo) Guiler. Since his appearance in *Henry and June*, he has been involved in a wide range of both mainstream and independent movie projects, many of which were adaptations of novels, such as *The Age of Innocence* (1993), *The Portrait of a Lady* (1996), and *Keep the Aspidistra Flying*, also known as *A Merry War* (1997). Kevin Spacey, who plays Richard Osborn, is a highly appreciated actor, probably best known for *American Beauty* (1999), for which he won both an Academy Award and BAFTA Award for Best Actor.

Kaufman's film bears the same title as the first volume of Nin's unexpurgated diary, but it diverges a great deal from it. First of all, Kaufman frequently condenses separate events of Nin's diary into one film sequence, thus distorting their original progression, setting, and context. For example, the book version of *Henry and June* opens with Nin talking to her cousin Eduardo in her Louveciennes house and expressing her need for "an older mind, a father, a stronger man than me, a lover who will lead me in love" (*Henry and June* 1). In Kaufman's version, this conversation is not the opening scene, and instead of Louveciennes, it takes place in a dressing room after Nin's dance class, which gives Kaufman an opportunity to display a scarcely clad de Medeiros/Nin.

Another example of diversion is the transformation of prose fragments of Nin's diary into dialogues. Although Nin recorded many conversations in her diary, Kaufman takes some of the reflective passages, not addressed to anyone, and changes them into dialogue. For instance, both in the film and in the movie such a line appears: "I have three desires now, to eat, to sleep and to fuck" (while, in the film, Nin does not actually say "fuck," it is clearly implied by the way she pauses and the following scene of lovemaking). While in the book this utterance is not addressed to anyone, in the film Nin says it to Miller. In the diary, Nin simply expresses her craving for more experience and a more intense existence, and Miller actually appears in this fragment as someone unable to meet these desires. Nin writes, "I want to bite into life, and be torn by it. Henry does not give me all this" (179). Therefore, the same sentence appears in totally different contexts.

Finally, Kaufman's Nin is largely a product of his own imagination, as many scenes in the film do not have equivalents in Nin's diary. For example, lesbian scenes were never so explicit and bold in Nin's published diaries. However, they are probable.

This is one reason why a faithful approach to this particular adaptation is largely redundant. Although the question "What shall we compare the film to?" may seem to produce a straightforward answer (to Nin's diary *Henry and June*), the answer ceases to be so simple when we consider the circumstances of the creation of Nin's unexpurgated diaries and the complexity of Nin's diaries in general. Nin's *Henry and June* was published in 1986, nine years after her death. Although Nin's partner, Rupert Pole, is listed as its official editor, the major editorial decisions were made by John Ferrone, who previously edited Nin's erotica. Ferrone, as correspondence between him and Pole reveals, was extremely hardnosed about the editing process. He wanted *Henry and June* to concentrate exclusively on Nin's relationship with Henry Miller and his wife June, and as a result, he made it into one of most coherent and un-journal-like of Nin's published diaries.* Commenting on *Henry and June* and comparing it to the first, expurgated volume of the *Diary*, which covers roughly the same years, critic Philip Jason notes, "reading them consecutively or even side-by-side, weaving back and forth between entries written about the same time, does not give readers the texture of the source or the evolving Nin we are seeking" (202). Consequently, rather than being "unexpurgated," *Henry and June* is differently expurgated and its role in conveying the "truthful" story of Anaïs Nin's life is rather ambiguous.

Furthermore, the volume *Henry and June* is just one of many various records of Nin's life available to the public today. There are the seven volumes of the *Diary of Anaïs Nin* (the first six of which were published during her lifetime); the four *Early Diaries* and the four unexpurgated volumes, all of which were published posthumously; and there are two English language biographies. None of these sources, however, tells the story of Nin's life as it was. Each is an assemblage of certain facts and interpretations of these facts. Each text constructs a different Nin and a different view of her life. Just as it is impossible to fix the meaning of any text, it is impossible to contain Nin and the story of her life. Even the original handwritten diary is a construction of Nin's life—writing down her experiences, she had to choose what to record and how to go about it. Although Nin's real life became an inspiration for many artistic creations (including Nin's own), it is impossible to determine once and for all the content and the meaning of her existence. We can only tell more stories. However, what is important is which story of her life is told and how it is told. So, the issue of fidelity is only of interest here in the sense Christopher Orr uses it, namely as "lapses of fidelity," or in other words, the changes made during adaptation, which "provide clues to ideology embedded in the [filmic] text" (Orr 73).

---

* *See "The Making of* Henry and June*, the book," in Vol. 4 of* A Café in Space: The Anaïs Nin Literary Journal *(2007).*

The second reason not to overly rely on the fidelity approach stems from adaptations studies themselves, which move away from the conventional fidelity approach because it is found to be too limited and too limiting. Reviewing recent literature on adaptations studies in *Literature/Film Reader: Issues of Adaptation* (2007), David M. Whaley indicates that many critics, including Peter Lev, Thomas Leitch, and David Kranz, encourage moving beyond the traditional issue of how faithfully a film reproduces the original literary source (Whaley 35). Instead, they grant a greater independence to film and suggest assessing it according to criteria specific to movie productions. At the same time, they do not ignore the direct source of a film altogether, but rather propose to examine it alongside other co-texts and contexts that contribute to the final product, such as other films, photographs, paintings, and/or historical events (35).

Kaufman's *Henry & June* is indeed an excellent example of a successful use of intertexts, since it is rich in intertextual references. Thanks to audio-visual possibilities of the movie, viewers can hear and see what can only be imagined when reading Nin's journal. For instance, Kaufman included musical pieces dating back to the beginning of the twentieth century, many of which were written by Nin's favorite composers, such as Debussy, Satie, and Chopin, whom she often praised in the pages of her diary.* Apart from exposing viewers to the music from the 1930s, Kaufman recreated the vintage atmosphere of Paris by incorporating original photographs by Brassaï and fragments of films that Nin mentioned in her diary, such as *La Passion de Jeanne D'Arc* (1928), *Un Chien Andalou* (1929) by Buñuel and Dalí, and *Maedchen in Uniform* (1931), which some recognize as the first lesbian picture. Kaufman also let the audience catch a glimpse of Nin's original childhood journal and a picture of an adolescent Nin.

Consequently, rather than asking how faithfully Nin's life is represented in Kaufman's film and how closely the film follows Nin's *Henry and June*, I propose investigating three questions: What is the role of the film in constructing Nin's public image?; How does eroticizing Nin in the film affect her image as a writer?; and, more broadly, Does Kaufman's representation of women and sexual acts reinforce or challenge certain stereotypes connected with femininity and sexuality? In order to answer these three questions, I examine some of Kaufman's choices: firstly, his choice to concentrate on this particular period of Nin's life; secondly, the way he creates Anaïs Nin as a character; thirdly, the frequent display of naked female bodies; and

---

* *Kaufman even included a piece by Nin's brother, Joaquín Nin-Culmell, who was a composer and pianist.*

finally, his construction of sexual scenes. Before I embark on this examination, I will provide an account of the change of an X rating into an NC-17 rating in the United States that accompanied the release of *Henry & June*. I will also comment on the reception of the movie in the press.

Although it was *The Right Stuff* that won Kaufman four Oscars, on the poster and in the trailer to *Henry & June*, he advertised himself as the director of *The Unbearable Lightness of Being*. Kaufman therefore addressed the portion of his audience who knew him for adapting Kundera's, rather than Wolfe's, book. It seems only natural as *Henry & June* is closer in both form and subject to *The Unbearable Lightness of Being*: both movies score high on sexual content. However, unlike *The Unbearable Lightness of Being*, which managed to get an R rating in the United States (which means that a person under 17 years old requires an accompanying parent or adult guardian), *Henry and June* initially received the feared X rating, which was later replaced by a new NC-17 category.

The movie rating system in the United States has been the domain of the Motion Picture Association of America (MPAA). The MPAA was founded in 1922, and its first president, Will Hays, established a set of rules for filmmakers, known as the Hays Code, which strictly and very specifically stated what could not be shown on the screen (for instance, no childbirth, or no criticism of religion). Films that followed the code were approved, and those that did not were disapproved ("Ratings History"). Then, in 1968, in the name of freedom of expression, Jack Valenti considerably modernized the rating system by introducing cautionary information about movies instead of deeming them as acceptable or unacceptable. Initially, the MPAA created a rating board that classified films as G (General Audience), M (Mature Audience—all ages admitted, but parental guidance suggested), R (Restricted—children under 16 admitted with a parent or adult guardian), and X (children under 17 will not be admitted).

Since then the rating system has undergone several modifications, one of which was introduced on September 26, 1990. It was a replacement of the X rating with the new NC-17 rating, which was really a change of name more than anything else. The X and NC-17 category stood for exactly the same thing—no one under 17 was admitted. Nonetheless, it helped to remove the stigma of the X rating, which had became associated with the pornography industry. Initially, the X category was supposed to signal adult content in a film. The first films released with an X rating, such as *Midnight Cowboy* (1969) or *A Clockwork Orange* (1971), were in no way negatively affected by the

X. In fact, the former even won an Oscar. However, as the X sign was not copyrighted, the pornography industry appropriated it freely, and soon "X" became synonymous with pornography. As a result, TV stations and newspapers refused to advertise any X rated movies, and major film studios obliged their directors to make movies that would meet the requirements of the R rating.

*Henry & June* was initially X rated, and this surprised the press, which generally agreed that although the film contained plenty of sexual scenes, they were rather tasteful. It was also felt that if Kaufman, one of the major film directors, was X rated, a change in the rating system was imminent. *Henry & June* was one of a few movies which received the X rating that year, and the *Los Angeles Times* called the year 1990 "The Year of the X" (Mathews "Oct. 3 Marks" 1). Other X rated films were the Spanish *Tie Me Up! Tie Me Down!*; the British *The Cook, the Thief, his Wife and her Lover*; and the American independent production *Life is Cheap...but toilet paper is expensive.* As the *Los Angeles Times* noted, "Most of the recent victims of the poisoned X have been relatively powerless independent filmmakers" (Mathews "Miller Meets the MPAA" 1).

*Henry & June*, although not exactly a mainstream production, was released with a major distributor, Universal Pictures. Since it was Universal Pictures policy not to release any films with an X rating, there were three options for Kaufman—to appeal the decision of the MPAA, to edit the movie to R rating standards, or to release the movie unrated with an independent distributor. Kaufman was supposed to appeal, but the MPAA modified the rating system the week before he would have, and as a result, *Henry & June* was the first recipient of the NC-17 rating. Although the alteration of the rating system was generally supported in the media, some did not fail to notice that it coincided with a major studio production (Universal Pictures was a member of the MPAA) (Mathews "Miller Meets MPAA" 1; Sterritt 10). Whatever motivated the MPAA to adjust the system, *Henry & June* became the face of the change.

The initial branding of *Henry & June* with an X rating and then the transformation of the X to an NC-17 were hotly debated in the press, and as a result Kaufman's film got extra publicity. The media discussed whether the introduced change was sufficient and whether it was fair that it had come together with a film released by Universal Pictures. They also reported on either sold-out shows, or movie theatres banning the film despite the new rating, as well as on newspapers, such as *Birmingham News* and *Sacramento Union*, which refused the advertising NC-17 films (Fox "'Henry and June' Ban" 1; Mathews

"Sell-out Crowds" 1; and *The San Francisco Chronicle*: "Alabama Paper" E5; "Second Newspaper" E11).

All major American newspapers and magazines related the unfolding events concerning the rating amendment. The *Los Angeles Times*, for instance, devoted eight articles to the rating change between August 27 and October 8, 1990, and *Henry & June* was mentioned in every single one, six times in the headlines. *The New York Times*, apart from the review of the film, featured eight articles concerning the dispute (between August 15 and December 15, 1990). *Henry & June* was brought up in all but two articles. Other major American newspapers, such as *USA Today*, the *Washington Post*, *The Washington Times*, *The Wall Street Journal*, *The Boston Globe*, *The Christian Science Monitor*, the *St. Louis Post-Dispatch*, the *Chicago Tribune*, and some popular magazines such as *Newsweek*, *Time*, and *Playboy*, ran at least one article on the issue, but usually more. The publication with the record number of articles on *Henry & June* and the rating change was, perhaps unsurprisingly, *The San Francisco Chronicle*. Unsurprisingly because San Francisco is not only Kaufman's home city but also home to a large gay community, which supported *Henry & June* from the very beginning.

When the film was originally X rated, the press reported that Kaufman had to adjust five scenes in order to get an R rating, among them, allegedly, three lesbian scenes (Mathews "Miller Meets the MPAA" 1). Kaufman believed that his film got an X because of an honest portrayal of a woman's sexual awakening, as he stated in *The San Francisco Chronicle* (Stone "A Director's Battle" 20). Gay and lesbian communities thought something different. The Gay and Lesbian Alliance against Defamation (GLAAD) suspected, as the *Los Angeles Times* reported, that the lesbian scenes in *Henry & June* resulted in an X rating. The GLAAD maintained that if the film contained comparable heterosexual acts, it would not have received such a rating, concluding that the film was unfairly given an X. Referring to the movie *Last Exit to Brooklyn*, which showed violence against homosexuals but nonetheless was R rated, the executive director of the GLAAD, Richard Jennings, commented to the Los Angeles newspaper, "The message we get is that it is OK to show gays and lesbians getting killed, but if you show them as complete individuals who have physical intimacy, you get an X" (Fox "Gays Call" 12).

What was of special interest to me while reading the articles on the change of the rating system was how Nin was described. The most striking misconception emerged in the headlines: It appeared that *Henry & June* is a film about Henry Miller rather than Anaïs Nin. Despite the fact that the movie was based on Nin's book, and despite the fact that Kaufman's intention was to portray Nin's sexual awakening, Nin's name does not appear in a single headline the way Miller's name does. For instance, the *Los Angeles Times* announced, "Henry Miller Meets the MPAA Movies: Philip Kaufman's very adult 'Henry and June,' a tale of the controversial author's days in Paris, apparently is the latest recipient of the dreaded X rating. Its U.S. release is in limbo" (Mathews 1). *The San Francisco Chronicle* also gives the impression that Miller is the main protagonist of the film, entitling their two articles "Philip Kaufman's story of Henry Miller ménage ran into problem" and "Henry Miller—On Trial Again?" (Stone F2). And while some of these articles give equal importance to Nin in the main text, others persist in their ignorance. For example, for Hal Hinson of the *Washington Post*, the movie is about "the American writer Henry Miller...and his wife, June...and their friend and lover, Anaïs Nin" (Hinson D1). He does not even acknowledge that the film is based on Nin's work.

So, the film got extra publicity, thanks to the change of the rating system. As far as reviews of the film are concerned, it got mixed assessments, many of them rather negative. The *Library Journal* did not recommend the movie, describing it as "pretentious, lifeless, and tiresome in the extreme" (137-8). Dave Kehr, in the *Chicago Tribune*, claimed that the film would be long remembered for changing the rating system, but the film itself had little to offer ("Philip Kaufman's *Henry & June* a glum copout"). Of a similar opinion was David Sterritt in *The Christian Science Monitor*, who stated, "In years to come, film-history books will state that 1990 saw the end of the X rating in its traditional form. A footnote will add that *Henry & June* was the first movie to arrive on-screen with the new "NC-17" label... Since this implies a small measure of immortality for *Henry & June*, it's too bad a more distinguished film didn't come along to inaugurate the new rating" (10). Furthermore, not a single review discussed how faithful (or not) the film is to Nin's book, which usually takes place when adaptations of literary works are evaluated. Not one reviewer commented on what was left out or what was added, which suggests that no one bothered to read the book which Kaufman used as his source.

Now, let us move on to examining Kaufman's choices, beginning with the first one: the period of Nin's life he decided to portray.

*Decision no.1: concentrating on this particular period of Nin's life*

Nin lived for seventy-three years, and it would be an understatement to say her life could be described as eventful. Kaufman decided to focus on her days in Paris in the early 1930s. He might have chosen to portray a different stage of Nin's existence—her childhood spent in various places in Europe and the abandonment by her father; her adolescence in a new country, America; the first years of her marriage and the move back to France; her escape to the U.S. at the beginning of World War II; her struggles to become a published writer; her numerous travels; or her successful years after the publication of the *Diary*. The choices are endless, and each of them has the potential to be an interesting story. Instead, Kaufman brought to screen Nin's relationship with June and Henry Miller. Why?

First of all, Philip Kaufman co-wrote the screenplay with his wife, Rose, and they both were fascinated with Nin and Miller, both of whom they had met in the 1960s, finding themselves transfixed. In the article for the *Boston Globe*, Kaufman admits that Miller's books inspired him to drop out of Harvard Law School and to live a freer existence, while Nin, during their encounter, encouraged him to get involved in filmmaking (Matthew 41). As a result, the Kaufmans had a very personal approach towards their subject, and the film can be regarded as a sort of tribute. Rose Kaufman, who initiated the idea to make *Henry and June* into a movie, recalls thus her first contact with Nin's unexpurgated diary:

> *Henry and June* sort of fell off the shelf over on Fillmore Street, at Browser Books, and I happened to have the time that night to read it, and I stayed up and finished it and got to bed about two or three in the morning. I was pretty wildly excited by it. And I felt, "maybe there's a film here." It was the revelation of these two people that we had known, had met, and had been inspired by. And then we were inspired all over again by their wild passion, particularly since there was this June element. (*Anaïs Nin: A Book of Mirrors* 265)

The film clearly sympathizes with Nin and Miller and it idealizes artistic creation, which is evident in a positive portrayal of the bohemian community, represented by Henry Miller, and it presents a rather unsympathetic portrayal of bourgeois society, represented by Nin's husband. While Miller is presented as a jaunty man, and Nin as a daring woman, Hugo is portrayed as a devoted, yet boring and prudish husband. For instance, in the scene where Nin and Miller engage in a fervent discussion about D.H. Lawrence and his representation of sexuality, an embarrassed Hugo keeps repeating, "We should eat something" (*H&J*). Kaufman also romanticizes bohemians by showing them as people who reject middle-class customs and mores and therefore are able to truly enjoy their lives.

However, apart from this personal fascination, there are other possible motives behind Kaufman's decision to adapt *Henry and June*. Kaufman was neither the first nor the last person to focus on this part of Nin's life. In fact, his film joins the tradition of texts which tell the story of Miller, Nin, and June. This trio gripped the imagination of their audience, and as a consequence, most plays on Nin refer to her years spent in Paris and recount the adventures of this ménage à trois. For instance, out of three plays which were staged after Nin's death and which got reviews in *The New York Times*, two were devoted to the Parisian period: *Anaïs Nin: The Paris Years* (1986) and *Anaïs Nin: One of Her Lives* (2006)*. The story of Miller, Nin, and June is appealing for at least two reasons. Firstly, it involves *two* well-known authors, which, for Kaufman, means that his movie can potentially attract the readers of both writers. Secondly, these two celebrities are entangled in a love affair, which gives Kaufman an opportunity to work in the popular genre of romance. So, although Kaufman could have chosen to focus on other stages of Nin's life, the choice he ultimately made was logical in that he had to take into consideration his prospective audience, who, at the end of the twentieth century, was obsessed with celebrity and love.

This trend is evident in a growing number of films devoted to the lives of famous writers. Although most of the stories told in cinema are appropriated from literary sources (Welsh xiii), since the 1990s, there have been a steady number of works—and lives—of popular writers turned into screenplays. Thus, apart from Anaïs Nin and Henry Miller in *Henry & June* (1990), we could follow the life of George Sand in *Impromptu* (1991), of C.S. Lewis in *Shadowlands* (1993), of Dorothy Parker in *Mrs. Parker and the Vicious Circle* (1994), of Oscar Wilde in *Wilde* (1997), of James Joyce in *Nora* (2000), of Sylvia Plath in *Sylvia* (2003), of Jane Austen in *Becoming Jane* (2007), and on and on. Most of these films feature a very prominent love theme, and the most extreme example of exploiting the love interest is *Becoming Jane*, which turns the life of the famous English spinster into a passionate love affair.

Therefore, it must be remembered that Kaufman's film presents only a very narrow part of Nin's life, and as a result, it introduces Nin to the film audience, and to Nin's potential readers, in a very particular way. First of all, it fossilizes Nin in a forever young and sexually adventurous pose, since the main concern of the film is Nin's sexual awakening. Secondly, it romanticizes the relationship between Henry

---

* *For a review of* Anaïs Nin: One of Her Lives, *see* A Café in Space, *Vol. 4, pp. 155-156—Ed.*

and Anaïs and ties them strongly together, an association that Nin managed to escape after the publication of her *Diaries* in 1966. How important Miller was for launching Nin's career can be seen in a letter Nin received from her husband Hugh Guiler in early 1965, when she was occupied with the publication of Miller's letters to her. Guiler wrote:

> Bay[*] offered $500 for your novel, or two of them, if he could get the Miller letters for $600. You remember Peter Owen[†] finally paid $2000 for the Miller letters and Gunther[‡] feels you should have at least $1500 for them from Bay. Also, he does not want him to be taking you only as a package with Miller, but feels he should be interested in doing your novels for their own sake... In general Gunther wants to stop anyone from taking you only as a package with Miller, which he thinks is not good for you. (HG to AN, Box 30; Folder 2)

Nin eventually managed to escape being treated as "a package with Miller," but the release of *Henry and June*, both the film and the diary, re-established the association. Consequently, her relationship with Henry Miller became one of the most recognizable "characteristics" of Nin. By repeating similar scenarios, texts such as *Henry and June* reduce Nin's life to time spent in Paris, and freeze Nin in a relationship with June and Henry Miller.

*Decision no. 2: creating Anaïs Nin as a character*

As for Kaufman's second choice—the way he portrays Nin—I am interested in what viewers, especially those who have never heard about Nin, find out about her from the movie. Let us consider the first few sequences and how Nin is introduced. In the first sequence, Nin is at a publisher's office, where she is discussing her book on D.H. Lawrence. However, the publisher is more interested in Nin herself rather than her book. He is curious how she came to know so much about sex, because, as he asserts, "you write about sex with such an authority" (*H&J*). Nin replies that her knowledge of sex came from literature and from erotic pictures she discovered in her new apartment. Nin sounds very naïve and innocent talking about her discovery with a childish enthusiasm. This sequence is a series of shot/reverse shots (Nin/the publisher) and a series of flashbacks to the discovery of the

---

[*] *André Bay was an editor of Editions Stock in Paris.*

[†] *Peter Owen was, and still is, Nin's publisher in the UK.*

[‡] *Gunther Stuhlmann was Nin's literary agent.*

pictures narrated with a voiceover. In the final shot of this sequence, the publisher enters the frame from the left, bends over and starts to kiss a rather confused Nin. It is a very unexpected turn of events, both for Nin and for the viewer.

In the third sequence, Nin writes in bed next to her sleeping husband. She wears a white, fluffy nightgown. The light is soft and reddish, and the scene is built up mostly from close-ups, which creates a sense of intimacy. While Nin writes in her diary, her voiceover simultaneously narrates what she records, which is the story of what really happened at the publisher's office. She relates how the man not only kissed her but also caressed her body, including her "most secret, sensitive part." Then Nin lifts her eyes from the diary, looks into the camera and says from the voiceover: "I tell Hugo only part of the story." The scene slowly fades out (*H&J*).

The film therefore introduces Nin as a writer, but at the same time, her writing is, from the very start, closely connected with sexuality. At the publisher's office she is not treated as a partner in business but as a sexual object. It is her body, and not her creation, that is desired. In the bedroom scene, Nin is established as a sort of "boudoir writer." Apart from one scene, close to the beginning of the movie, in which Nin is seen at the typewriter, she is mainly encountered writing in bed. There is also a scene in which she writes at the balcony while Henry and Hugo play the French game of "boules," which again suggests that for Nin writing is a mere pastime, a leisure rather than profession. While the men spend their free time playing, Nin spends it "scribbling" in her diary. This presentation of Nin's writing as a leisure activity distorts the image Nin herself promotes in her diaries. Firstly, as far as her diary writing is concerned, Nin talked about the diary as an "opium habit" (*Diary 1* 312, 319), her drug and vice (*Diary 2* 322). She gave an impression of urgency, describing her writing thus: "The pale winter sun is shining on what I write. I write while I wait for patients. I write after they leave, I write while eating my dinner, at times instead of dinner. I write lying down on a rust-colored bedspread" (27). Secondly, during that period Nin did attempt to write fiction, yet in the film she is portrayed mainly as a diary writer.

Kaufman's presentation of Nin's writing as a leisure activity in the film becomes particularly evident when contrasted with the presentation of Miller's writing. When Nin writes, she does so in bed and the voiceover makes her thoughts "audible," which creates intimacy and provides spectators with an insight into her secrets. It is due to the fact that Nin is pictured writing the diary and not fiction. When Miller writes, he does so in an artistic frenzy at the typewriter, smoking cigarettes, and sometimes writing continuously for days. The audience does not get to "hear" his thoughts: the only sound accompanying him is the clicking of the typewriter. However, the viewers can see the results of his labor—the mounting pile of typewritten pages. What is more, most scenes in Miller's house take place around his workplace, at the desk with his typewriter and various notes pinned to the wall. At Nin's house, most of the action and writing takes place in bed.

Although Kaufman does present Nin as a writer, her writing and the progress of her ideas become secondary. *Henry & June*, as a Hollywood production, follows certain classical rules of the Hollywood narrative style, according to which a plot of the film should have "a clear forward direction," and it should concentrate on a small number of characters whose goals should be established at the beginning of the film and achieved at the end of it (Lehman and Luhr 29). Thus, the main storyline of the film is Nin's sexual awakening and her relationship with Henry and June. Kaufman got rid of, for instance, Nin's psychoanalysis and stripped Nin of many dilemmas regarding her affairs. He therefore condensed further the already condensed diary. The first scenes of the film establish Nin as a sexually curious, yet not very experienced, person. Upon meeting Henry and June, she begins to explore the realm of sexuality. The movie ends with Nin's breaking from both June and Henry and a voiceover monologue in which she states, "That morning...I wept because the process by which I had become a woman was painful" (*H&J*). It is therefore the woman, rather than the artist, which is of greater interest to Kaufman.

*Decision no. 3: the frequent display of naked female bodies*

Moving on to examining the third of Kaufman's decisions, I question his frequent display of naked women. Throughout the film, women's bodies are shown more frequently, for longer periods of time, and are more revealed than male bodies. For instance, there are three separate scenes which take place in a brothel, and, as can be expected, in each of them there is an abundance of naked women. Although Kaufman can be credited with presenting a variety of women's bodies, in many different shapes, colors and sizes, therefore challenging the ideal body type, he has to be criticized for romanticizing brothels. Brothels in Kaufman's film—unlike their real-life counterparts, which are places of exploitation—are cozy, filled with cigarette smoke and nostalgic music. Prostitutes, supervised by a friendly, if a little bit greedy, elderly Madam, seem content.

Although naked men do occasionally appear in the movie, they are not eroticized in the same way as women. First of all, men are naked only in the scenes which require them to be so (i.e. lovemaking scenes).

It is not the same for women. In addition to brothel sequences, where many naked female bodies are on display, there are also a few scenes involving Nin, in which nudity is present just for nudity's sake. In one of these, Nin lies passively on her back, stark naked, looking into the camera. Only her bent knee prevents us from seeing, as Nin puts it, "her most secret, sensitive part." This scene is framed like a picture; there is no movement; only Nin's voiceover is audible. As Laura Mulvey explains, cinema offers a number of pleasures, one of which is scopophilia—pleasure in looking (Mulvey 2184). Thus exposed, Nin is here clearly to satisfy viewers' pleasure.

Women are also eroticized by the clothes they wear in the movie. Nin, June, and women in the brothel often wear lingerie, through which we can see their bodies. Whenever we see Nin writing, she is clad in some kind of feminine negligee. There are also a few scenes of a fully dressed man and a skimpily dressed woman. One such scene takes place at the beginning of the movie, when Nin, wearing just a slip, talks to her fully-clad cousin Eduardo. Another one, probably more significant, is half-way through the movie, when Miller visits Nin upon completing his book, *Tropic of Cancer*. He comes into Nin's room, looks at her (and so does the camera) dressed in a black, long, lace, see-through negligee, takes out his manuscript, puts it on the shelf, and says "finished." He then goes towards Nin and starts kissing her passionately. The sequence preceding this one shows Miller as an inspired artist with a cigarette dangling from his mouth frantically typing at his typewriter. Continuous fade-ins and fades-outs suggest passing time. There is no indication as to what Nin does with her time when Miller works. But the movie suggests that not much, as Nin does not have any writing of her own to show him. She just seems to be waiting for her men, looking impeccable in her sexy outfit and carefully applied make-up.

The display of female bodies in films is closely connected with the issue of gaze. According to Laura Mulvey, in the patriarchal society,

> pleasure in looking has been split between active/male and passive/female. The determining male gaze projects its fantasy onto a female figure, which is styled accordingly. In the traditional exhibitionist role women are simultaneously looked at and displayed with their appearance coded for a strong visual and erotic impact so that they can be said to connote to-be-looked-at-ness. (2186).

Since Kaufman's film is based on Nin's diary, we can expect the story to be filmed from her point of view: she should be the one to hold the gaze. But does she? She does, but not always. Nin is looked at as much as she is looking. Besides two already mentioned scenes (one, the naked Nin in bed narrating the events from voiceover; two, Miller watching Nin in the black negligee), there are plenty more in which Nin becomes an object of desire. For example, there are three scenes in which Nin dances. First, there is the dancing class scene in which Nin practices flamenco. She is closely watched by her male teacher and also by her cousin, who, shortly after, confesses his love for her. Then, there is a scene in the bar in which Nin dances seductively in front of Miller. He looks her up and down through squinted eyes, and shortly thereafter their first sexual encounter takes place. Miller comments that he saw her true nature when she was dancing. The third dancing scene again happens in the bar. This time Nin is with her husband. As they dance, Nin, tilting her head coquettishly, is watched, or rather visually devoured, by all men who set their eyes on her.

Although there are several scenes in which Nin is indeed "the bearer of the look" (Mulvey), her gaze does not challenge the social order. In one of these scenes, Nin plays the voyeur as she observes June and Miller kissing in her living room. In another, she and her husband watch an enactment of sexual intercourse performed by two prostitutes. This scene, however, is ambiguous and can be interpreted in at least two different ways. On the one hand, simply by being in a brothel, Nin transgresses the social norm that a brothel is a place suitable for men, but not for women. Moreover, by ordering a woman to "stop pretending to be a man," and taking pleasure from looking at women satisfying each other, Nin's gaze challenges heterosexual desire. On the other hand, Nin can be regarded as taking on a masculine role and appropriating a typically masculine gaze. In a way, Nin objectifies these women as men do, by ordering them around and paying for their performance. It seems like another missed opportunity to challenge the scopophilic male gaze.

*Decision no. 4: construction of sexual scenes*

As far as the way Kaufman constructs erotic scenes is concerned, the film both challenges and reinforces some stereotypes concerning sexuality and sex. Kaufman presents a variety of sexual scenes, and each is filmed differently. There are close-ups, slow motion, and a wide range of lighting conditions. Scenes of sexual intercourse are by no means graphic. The depiction of sex is rather arty, and perhaps that is why the press was indignant when the film was given an X rating.

Kaufman includes two scenes in which a woman receives cunnilingus, thus focusing on female sexual pleasure. He also shows Miller to be impotent in one scene, which challenges the myth of masculine virility. Yet, the main contribution of the film to defy the mainstream portrayal of sexuality is the exploration of homoerotic desire. As mentioned before, *Henry & June* was supported by a gay and lesbian media watchdog, which suggests that the homosexual community welcomed the film's representation of homosexuality. The homosexual desire is portrayed through a few relationships in the movie: between Nin and June, June and her American friend Jean, and two prostitutes.

The relationship of Nin and June obviously receives the most attention. The first scene to hint at the desire between the two women takes place in the cinema. Anaïs and June, together with their husbands, watch the German film *Maedchen in Uniform*, controversial in the thirties, and noted as one of the first movies with a lesbian storyline. Kaufman therefore skillfully weaves in a very suggestive clue. The scene screened shows a female teacher in the dormitory kissing young girls goodnight. June whispers to Nin, "You're like the schoolteacher. I'm like the young girl," and then takes Nin's hand, which does not escape the attention of Nin's husband. Then, before June's departure to New York, the two friends go to a lesbian bar. They drink, converse, embrace, dance, and finally kiss passionately (*H&J*).

June is not, however, the only person whom Nin desires. Shortly after June leaves for New York, Nin begins an affair with Henry. Throughout the film, Nin is attracted to various people: June, Henry, a prostitute, Nin's husband, and her cousin Eduardo. The film, therefore, presents desire as complex. Queer theorists argue that we cannot classify or fix desire. Noreen Giffney explains queer theory in relation to identity and desire: "It signifies the messiness of identity, the fact that desire and thus the desiring subject cannot be placed into discrete identity categories, which remain static for the duration of people's lives" (Giffney 9). The film plays with this idea by challenging the unity and stability of desire. However, the credit for this should be probably given to Nin rather than Kaufman. Despite the controversy that went into editing the volume, the diary *Henry and June* provides a very insightful exploration of ambiguous human emotions. Nin captures the contradictory feelings experienced by a couple: on the one hand, there is a desire to maintain the illusion of eternal love; on the other hand, there is a craving for more varied sexual experiences. Nin also records the feelings of hate and love directed towards the same person, the need to belong and the need to be free.

There are, however, some elements of the film that strongly perpetuate stereotypes about sex. Particularly disturbing fragments of the film occur when Nin is coerced into sexual intercourse, first by Miller and then by her husband. The first sexual encounter between Nin and Miller in the movie, unlike in Nin's diary, takes place in the bar, behind the stage where the musicians are playing pulsating music on bongo drums. Miller meets Nin in the corridor, lifts her in his arms, carries her backstage and places her on the table. While Nin lies on her back, Miller climbs over her. There is a tussle between them, as Nin tries to resist him. Referring to her seductive dance in front of him earlier, Miller asks her, "You want to dance?" and as he starts making love to her, he says, "Dance!" (*H&J*). Miller is very decisive and determined to get what he wants. He orders Nin to open her legs wider, at which point Nin gives in, embraces Miller and starts to moan. The music accompanying the scene is getting louder and faster, suggesting climax.*

Another scene in which Nin is forced into sex (or we can even say raped, because despite the fact that the sequence is more stylish than usual rape scenes, in the end, it is just that) takes place during the student ball. Nin walks alone through a crowd of loud, half naked people (n. b. more naked women than men) celebrating on the streets of Paris. She is followed by a man in a rather scary mask, but she is completely oblivious. When Nin spots a man with a bear, she turns into a side street to follow him. She arrives in a courtyard where she observes a black man playing African percussion and naked women dancing by a fire. As Nin watches them, the man who has followed her grabs her suddenly from behind. They scuffle, Nin puts up a fight, but he forces himself on her. Nin tries to resist him, but as he rapes/makes love to her, she seems to start to enjoy the experience. Finally, the man whispers, "I love you, Pussywillow," which is Nin's husband's nickname for her (*H&J*). Both Nin and the audience can sigh with a relief: It is only her husband (although Nin sighs more with pleasure than relief). This sequence is very unsettling, since it remains unknown till the very end who has attacked Nin. In the next scene Nin records what has just took place in her diary, as usual, in bed. She admits enjoying the experience and says, "My first infidelity to Henry was with my own husband. I've changed. I feel restless... I want pleasure" (*H&J*).

These two sequences reinforce several stereotypes about rape: firstly, that a woman cannot be raped by a person close to her; secondly, that a woman enjoys violent sex; thirdly, that a woman "was asking for it" by being seductive. Interestingly, neither of these two scenes has an equivalent in the book version of *Henry and June*. For example, according to Nin's diary, her first sexual encounter with

---

* *This scene is, however, later paralleled by another in which Nin is the seductress. Just as Miller has seduced her, she now seduces Eduardo. This time Nin initiates sexual intercourse. She places Eduardo on the table and climbs on him, whispering, "I want to show you things. I want to teach you things."*

Miller took place in Miller's hotel room and was as much the fulfillment of her desire as his. Moreover, these rape scenes employ very clichéd metaphors for sexual passion. When Hugo rapes Anaïs, we can hear the African drums playing louder and louder, and the camera switches between Hugo and Nin to the naked women dancing to the wild drums by the fire. This link between sexual desire and African tribal ceremonies not only exploits very worn-out imagery, but also strengthens the stereotype of unrestrained and primitive black sexuality.

I will provide answers to three originally posed questions: What is the role of the film in constructing Nin's public image?; How does eroticizing Nin in the film affect her image as a writer?; and Does Kaufman's representation of women and sexual acts reinforce or challenge certain stereotypes connected with femininity and sexuality?

First of all, Kaufman's film played an important role in constructing Nin's public image. Because it got so much attention in the media upon its release due to a (coincidental) change in the rating system, it introduced Nin to new audiences. It is highly probable that many people back then, and perhaps even now, saw/see Nin first before they read her. Potentially, this can have both positive and negative effects on Nin's legacy as a writer.

On the one hand, the film can possibly encourage people to read Nin, as was the case for at least one self-described non-reader, for whom the film marked the beginning of the fascination with Nin and Miller. He is quoted as saying, "As the credits rolled, I discovered that this Henry Miller and Anaïs Nin weren't fictional characters—they were real people who had written books about what we'd just seen! I was chomping at the bit—I had to buy this *Tropic of Cancer* and the *Diary*, and there wasn't a moment to lose!" The film, therefore, has the potential to revive Nin and bring her to the attention of a new group of readers.

On the other hand, if viewers find the film unsuccessful, they may be discouraged from ever attempting to read any of Nin's writings. Sara Martin, who conducted an informal study on how film adaptations of *Wuthering Heights* influence the readers'/viewers' image of Heathcliff, found that "Audiences familiar with Brontë's novel, consider...the performances [of Heathcliff by various actors] in relation to whether they fit the way they mentally 'perform' Heathcliff as readers. However, if the novel is read or reread after seeing the film, the reader's visual representation of Heathcliff will be inevitably colored to a greater or lesser degree—or even dominated—by the actor spectators feel best succeeded in the role" (Martin 54). Since there is just one "biopic" of Nin's life, there is a chance that spectators of *Henry & June* will only reach for Nin's books if they find the character played by de Medeiros likable.

As for the answer to the second question—How does eroticizing Nin in the film affect her image as a writer?—I believe that the film presents a highly sexualized image of Nin, thus diminishing her role as a writer. This eroticized image of Nin clashes with an image she created for herself during her lifetime by carefully editing her *Diaries*. Nin presented herself mainly as an artist (although we can never know whether she would have approved of the editing of the *Henry and June* diary). The film therefore contributes to the process of eroticization of Nin, which began with the publication of her first "unexpurgated" diary, *Henry and June*, in 1986. Since then there has been a great emphasis on Nin's sexual affairs, rather than on her literary achievement. For example, in 1987 *A Literate Passion: Letters of Anaïs Nin and Henry Miller, 1932-1953* was released, which again focused on the personal side of the Nin-Miller relationship. In the words of the editor, Gunther Stuhlmann, "Space limitations...made it necessary to eliminate material peripheral to the personal story—lengthy discussions of Dostoevsky, Proust, Joyce, D.H. Lawrence; detailed critiques of one another's work-in-progress; ruminations on films, books and so on" (xix). Three years after the release of the movie, the first biography of Nin was published, under the suggestive title *The Erotic Life of Anaïs Nin* (1993), and enfolded other love affairs, infidelities, and romances of the writer.

As far as the movie's potential to challenge cultural stereotypes regarding femininity and sexuality, Kaufman succeeds in some respects but fails in others. On the one hand, the film is an interesting exploration of desire, and its representation of homosexual relationships was approved by gay communities. On the other hand, the frequent exhibition of naked, eroticized women throughout Kaufman's movie blatantly depicts women as sexual objects. Moreover, some scenes of sexual intercourse, intended to be erotic, legitimize rape. ◈

*Works Cited*

---

Associated Press. "Alabama Paper Refuses Ads for NC-17 Film." *The San Francisco Chronicle*. 12 Oct. 1990. p. E5. *NewsBank* Web. 12 Sept. 2009.

----. "Second Newspaper Bans Ads for NC-17 Movies." *The San Francisco Chronicle*. 16 Oct. 1990. p. E11. *NewsBank* Web. 12 Sept. 2009.

Fox, David J. "Gays Call X Rating for 'Henry and June' a Stigma. Movies: Media watchdog group says the label is unfair. Universal Pictures plans to appeal." *Los Angeles Times*. 11 Sept. 1990. p. 12. ProQuest. Web. 10 Sept. 2009.

----. "'Henry & June' Ban Called an 'Isolated Situation'." *Los Angeles Times*. 6 Oct. 1990. p1. ProQuest. Web. 10 Sept. 2009.

Giffney, Noreen. "The 'q' word." Eds. Noreen Giffney and Michael O'Rourke. *The Ashgate Research Companion to Queer Theory*. Aldershot: Ashgate. 2009.

Guiler, Hugh. A Letter to Anaïs Nin. 1965. Nin Archive. Box 30; Folder 2.

Hinson, Hal. "'Henry & June': Hot & Daring." *The Washington Post*. 5 Oct.1990. p. D1. *LexisNexis*. Web. 12 Sept. 2009.

Jason, Philip K. "Dropping Another Veil: Anaïs Nin's *Henry and June*." Ed. Philip K. Jason. *The Critical Response to Anaïs Nin*. Westport: Greenwood Press. 1996. 199-204.

Kaufman, Philip, dir. *Henry & June*. Perf. Maria de Medeiros, Uma Thurman, and Fred Ward. 1990. Universal Pictures. DVD.

Kaufman, Philip and Rose Kaufman. "On 'Henry & June': The Making of the Movie." Ed. Paul Herron. *Anaïs Nin: A Book of Mirrors*. Huntington Woods: Sky Blue Press. 1996. 264-8.

Kehr, David. Review of *Henry & June*. "Philip Kaufman's 'Henry & June' A Glum Copout." *Chicago Tribune*. 5 Oct. 1990. Friday sect. p. 1. NewsBank. Web. 12. Sept. 2009.

Lehman, Peter and William Luhr. *Thinking About Movies: Watching, Questioning, Enjoying*. 2nd ed. Oxford: Blackwell Publishing. 2003.

Martin, Sara. "What does Heathcliff Look Like? Performance in Peter Kosminky's Version of Emily Brontë's *Wuthering Heights*." Ed. Mireia Aragay. *Books in Motion: Adaptation, Intertextuality, Authorship*. Amsterdam: Rodopi. 2005. 51-67.

Mathews, Jack. "Henry Miller Meets the MPAA; Movies: Philip Kaufman's very adult 'Henry and June,' a tale of the controversial author's days in Paris, apparently is the latest recipient of the dreaded X rating. Its U.S. release is in limbo." *Los Angeles Times* 27 Aug. 1990. p. 1. *ProQuest*. Web. 10 Sept. 2009.

----. "Oct. 3 Marks the Spot for Movie Showdown Ratings: Universal will appeal the X given to 'Henry & June' next month. Theatre owners are said to balk at a new category." *Los Angeles Times*. 15 Sept. 1990. p. 1. *ProQuest*. Web. 10 Sept. 2009.

----. "Sell-Out Crowds for 'Henry and June'; Movies: The controversy over the new adults-only NC-17 rating also draws protesters in Santa Ana." *Los Angeles Times*. 8 Oct. 1990. p. 1. *ProQuest*. Web. 10 Sept. 2009.

Matthew, Gilbert. "Behind the X Appeal: Spirit, sexuality lured Kaufman into his film 'Henry and June'." *The Boston Globe*. 5 Oct. 1990. p. 41. *LexisNexis*. Web. 11 Sept. 2009.

"Motion Picture Association of America." *Encyclopaedia Britannica.* 2010. CD-ROM.

Mulvey, Laura. "Visual Pleasure and Narrative Cinema." Eds. Vincent B. Leitch et al. *The Norton Anthology of Theory and Criticism.* London: W.W. Norton and Company. 2001. 2181-92.

Nin, Anaïs. *Henry and June.* London: Penguin Books. 1990.

----. *The Journal of Anaïs Nin: Volume 1.* Ed. Gunther Stuhlmann. London: Quartet Books. 1973.

----. *The Journal of Anaïs Nin: Volume 2.* Ed. Gunther Stuhlmann London: Quartet Books. 1974.

Orr, Christopher. "The Discourse of Adaptation: A Review." *Wide Angle.* 6 (2). 1984. 72-6.

Pennington, Jody W. *The History of Sex in American Film.* London: Praeger. 2007.

Pitman, Randy. Review of *Henry and June.* "Henry & June." *The Library Journal.* 15 April 1990. 137-8.

"Ratings History." MPPA.org Motion Picture Association of America. 2010. Web. 10 Nov. 2010.

Sterritt, David. "'Henry & June': First NC-17 Flick is a Dud." *The Christian Science Monitor.* 10 Oct. 1990. p. 10. *LexisNexis.* Web. 12 Sept. 2009.

Stone, Judy. "A Director's Battle Over Rating. Philip Kaufman's story of Henry Miller ménage ran into problem." *The San Francisco Chronicle.* 30 Sept. 1990. p. 20. *LexisNexis.* Web. 12 Sept. 2009.

----. "Henry Miller—On Trial Again? Kaufman's new movie unofficially given an X rating." *The San Francisco Chronicle.* 27 Aug. 1990. p. F2. *LexisNexis.* Web. 12 Sept. 2009.

Stuhlmann, Gunther, Ed. *A Literate Passion: Letters of Anaïs Nin and Henry Miller 1932-1953.* San Diego: Harcourt Brace and Company. 1987.

Welsh, James M. "Introduction: Issues of Screen Adaptation: What is Truth?" Eds. James M. Welsh and Peter Lev. *Literature/Film Reader: Issues of Adaptation.* Plymouth: The Scarecrow Press, Inc. 2007. xiii-xxvii.

Whaley, David M. "Adaptation Studies and the History of Ideas: The Case of Apocalypse Now." Eds. James M. Welsh and Peter Lev. *Literature/Film Reader: Issues of Adaptation.* Plymouth: The Scarecrow Press, Inc. 2007. 35-50.

*Satoshi Kanazawa*

## Multiplying Women

*Reflection, repetition and multiplication in the works of Maya Deren and Anaïs Nin*

*The Encounter of Two Women*

In the summer of 1944, when she and her friends were taking a walk on the beach of Amagansett, New York, Anaïs Nin encountered a strange scene. A woman was lying on the shore, letting herself be pummeled by the waves while two people filmed it.[1] Later, Nin found out the woman was Maya Deren, an avant-garde filmmaker, who was filming the opening scene of *At Land* (1945). After this meeting, the two female artists, both of whom were struggling underground figures, forged an enduring relationship, which one Nin biographer would later describe as a "rivalry" (Fitch 279).

In terms of age, at least, the word "rivalry" seems somewhat inappropriate because at forty-one, Nin was fourteen years older than Deren. In 1945, Nin saw Deren's first works, *Meshes of the Afternoon* (1944) and the finished version of *At Land*, and admired her talent, comparing her to Jean Cocteau. Because of Deren's youthful, incendiary energy, it was inevitable that Nin would get involved with her filmmaking.

Although she released only a handful of short silent films, Maya Deren is now hailed as a pioneer in American avant-garde filmmaking. Few books on film history fail to note her name. But, in a sense, Deren was an amateur director. Before she became a filmmaker, she was a poet. When she was younger, she wanted to be a dancer, or a singer, and it was the Czech filmmaker Alexander (Sasha) Hammid who introduced her to the world of film. They married in 1943, and then they shot *Meshes of the Afternoon* at their new place on Kings Road in Hollywood. The film, in which the two were both cast and crew, was shot exclusively by themselves. Although the film was only made for private use, it became as highly regarded as the surrealistic works of Cocteau, Salvador Dalí, or Luis Buñuel, and was awarded the 1947 Cannes Film Festival's "Grand Prix International for 16mm Film, Experimental Class."

Deren's work sheds light on the advantage amateurs have over professionals. An amateur is, in its Latin meaning, a "lover" of something. While the professional artist is fettered by economic realities and marketability, the amateur takes action purely on the grounds of love for the object. Therefore, amateurs are free (Deren 17).

It seems quite natural that Nin, who formed an anti-commercial literary circle with Henry Miller and other writers in Paris in 1930s, had an affinity for Deren's amateurism.

In a June 1945 entry in her diary, Nin made a remark on Deren's works: "Truly unconscious dream material, better in some ways than the early surrealist movies because there are no artificial effects, just a simple following of the threads of fantasy... I see the influence of Cocteau, except that she will not resort to any symbolism or artifice to present the dream. The dream resembles realism. The objects are not altered, there is no mystery. There is nothing to indicate that one is dreaming or free-associating. A curious prosaic quality imposed upon the imagination" (*Diary 4* 67-68).

Although these remarks were first published some twenty years later, they are among the earliest referring to Deren's work. Nin's insight was accurate, for she pointed out that Deren's works were prosaic, not poetic, and realistic. Generally speaking, one would expect quite the reverse to be expressed. Just as realism is supposed to represent reality as it is, Deren's works represent the dream as it is, according to Nin, without any artificial distortion.

With all this appreciation from the very beginning, why did Nin become displeased with Deren? One could conclude, in a prosaic, biographic manner, that it was simply because Nin was dissatisfied with her screen appearance in Deren's *Rituals in Transfigured Time* (1946). However, their relationship was so intricate that we do it disservice with such a dismissal. Mirrors, above all, will be the key to this study—I will examine how the two female artists respectively represented the role of mirrors and the reflection of self-image.

*Multiplying Women*

The three most outstanding of Deren's short films, *Meshes of the Afternoon, At Land*, and *Rituals in Transfigured Time*, remind us of Buñuel's 1930s surrealism. With only these three 15-minute silent movies, she paved the way for new expression by younger filmmakers such as Jonas Mekas, John Cassavetes, Martin Scorsese, and David Lynch. The consistent theme of these works is the splitting and multiplication of the Self. How the Self, which is essentially supposed to be "one," is transformed into "many" is superbly documented through dreamlike images. Here we will see the process of repetition/ splitting/multiplication by exploring the structure of the most suspenseful of the three, *Meshes of the Afternoon.*

*Meshes of the Afternoon* consists of 161 shots, according to Deren's own count (Clark 85-94). These shots are, on the whole, divided into five sequences.

The first sequence, from shot number 1 to 27, which we call here "sequence A," goes like this: At the walkway of a house with a Mediterranean look, someone deposits a flower. A shadow of a girl picks up the flower. The girl runs after the other figure but cannot catch up with it. She gives up pursuing, takes the stairway and steps into the room. In the empty room, there is a hint that someone has been there just before. After going upstairs, the girl sits in a chair by the window. There is a close-up of an eye, which eventually closes.

What is characteristic of sequence A is that the girl does not appear on the screen, and what the audience sees is composed from the first-person viewpoint of the girl. Her eye is shot in a close-up in shot 27, but her whole figure has never been introduced. When the sleepy eye is closed, one might expect that the whole thing would happen in her dream.

The next sequence, from shot 28 to 60, is the repetition and variation of sequence A. The camera captures the outside view, where the figure is walking. The figure is clothed in black, whose face is nothing but a mirror. Even though the "mirror" is walking very slowly, the running girl cannot catch up with it. She gives up pursuing and takes the stairway. At this moment (shot 37), the full visage of the girl, played by Maya Deren, appears for the first time. The act of opening the door and going upstairs is performed for a variation. The girl sees her double sleeping in the chair. She approaches the window, looking out onto the road. Up to this point, the second sequence has repeated the course of time in sequence A, so we can call the shots from 28 to 60 "sequence A'."

In terms of repetitions and variations, the structure of *Meshes of the Afternoon* is analyzable into the following five sequences:

A - A' - A'' - A''' - B

Until the final sequence B, time does not progress and the exploration of the dream world is repeated. And, as is shown in the first repetition, the girl played by Deren is not one person. She is continually multiplying.

In sequence A'' (from shot 61 to 97), the double stands beside the sleeping girl, looking out onto the road, where we can see another girl running after the "mirror." In her shot list, Deren counts the second girl as "dream girl no. 1" and the third girl "dream girl no. 2." When the "mirror" has gone away and the third girl gives up pursuing, she repeats the act of opening the door. In the room, the "mirror" is carrying a flower. The third girl is perplexed. The "mirror" deposits the flower on the bed, and then disappears. The flower is replaced by a knife. The first girl is still sleeping beside the bed. "Dream girl no. 2" looks out of the window.

In Sequence A''', the last repetitive sequence (from shot 98 to 154), the tension rises to its highest level. "Dream girl no. 3" is pursuing the "mirror" on the road outside. She gives up pursuing, climbs up the stairway, and enters the house. At last, the three dream girls confront each other. "Dream girl no. 3" is slightly aggressive. The three girls start a "conference" concerning the key and the knife. "Dream girl no. 1" and "dream girl no. 2" are so suspicious that they throw a hostile, languorous glance at "dream girl no. 3." (Shot 112, Fig. 1) The sleeping girl is still in the chair, stirring as if in a nightmare. "Dream girl no. 3" holds the knife, wears strange glasses (which Deren describes as "mirror eyes"), and then, in a determined manner, strides toward the sleeping girl. "Dream girl no. 3" is ready to plunge the knife into the sleeping girl. And then, "dream girl no. 3" is replaced by a man. The man, played by Hammid, displays a lover's intimacy and deposits a flower on the bed, just as the "mirror" has done. He reaches out his hand to caress her. The flower changes into a knife, the girl opens her eyes and takes the knife to resist him. The man's face, which turns out to be a mirrored reflection, is shattered. The pieces of the shattered mirror fall into the sands on the seashore.

Fig. 1. "Shot 112" from *Meshes of the Afternoon*

Sequence B (from Shot 155 to 161) depicts the events after the varied A sequences. Walking up from the road and through the stairway is filmed again, but this time it is the man who climbs up the stairway. When he enters the room, he finds the girl sitting in the chair, bleeding to death.

With all this analysis of the shots, we cannot come close to the mysteriousness of *Meshes of the Afternoon.* What we ascertained here is not the mystery, but the clarity of the work. It is quite clear that each repetition multiplies the Self. Sequence A, which adopted the first-person viewpoint, is not mysterious enough to dispel its reality. In this sequence, the black-clad figure does not reveal its mirrored face, and the mysteriousness of the mirrored figure's inapproachability is restrained. Only in the dream sequences from A' to A''' do the surrealistic and mysterious qualities develop. Between the realistic sequences A and B, the repetitions of the dream are inserted.

As for the later works, *At Land* and *Rituals in Transfigured Time*, it will be sufficient to say, in order to avoid a prolonged discussion, that these are, to some extent, the repetitions and variations of the theme and technique of *Meshes of the Afternoon.* In these works, each woman played by Deren continues multiplying.

*Against the Mirror*

Why does the Self multiply in the works of Maya Deren? To answer this question, it is quite clear, especially in *Meshes of the Afternoon*, that the mirror plays a crucial role. Who is the "mirror," and why does the destruction of the "mirror" cause the death of the Self? One might expect to find a psychoanalytic implication in the symbolic items placed in this work: a flower, a key, and a knife. Beginning with an interpretation of these items and referring to the mirror stage may seem to point toward a plausible explanation, but the fact is, however, that Deren denied that there were any psychoanalytic implications in her work. "A flower...is a flower, a mirror is a mirror, a knife is a knife" (*Diary 6* 351). Some critics, including Nin, pointed out that Deren's denial was actually a revolt against her father, Solomon Deren, who, while not a Freudian psychiatrist, was nonetheless involved with the treatment of "mentally defective" children (Clark 108). It is quite fair to say that Deren's revolt against psychoanalysis anticipates Susan Sontag's 1960s essay "Against Interpretation," in which Sontag challenges the modern style of interpretation, saying that by "reducing art to its content, and then interpreting *that*, one tames the work of art. Interpretation makes art manageable, comfortable" (Sontag 7-8), thus degrading art into the bourgeois collection of knowledge.[2]

Anaïs Nin was also an artist who persistently stuck to the mirror concept. She called her lifelong diary her mirror, and she confessed to Otto Rank that she "felt like a shattered mirror." (*Diary 1* 273) Henry

Miller reflected on what the mirror meant for Nin in "Un Être Étoilique" (1939), which also would shed light on Deren's mirror. Miller compares the artist who delves into his/her consciousness in order to realize the world to "Jonah in the belly of the whale." His assertion on the characteristic of Nin's diary is as follows:

> The person who is doing this [Nin] is really an innocent little creature tucked away in the lining of the belly of the whale. In nullifying herself she really becomes this great leviathan which swims the deep and devours everything in sight. It is a strange *dédoublement* of the personality in which the crime is related back to the whale by a sort of self-induced amnesia. There, tucked away in a pocket of the great intestinal tract of the whale, she dreams away throughout whole volumes of something which is not the whale, of something greater, something beyond which is nameless and unseizable. She has a little pocket mirror which she tacks up on the wall of the whale's intestinal gut and into which she gazes for hours on end. The whole drama of her life is played out before the mirror. If she is sad the mirror reflects her sadness; if she is gay the mirror reflects her gayety. But everything the mirror reflects is false, because the moment she realizes that her image is sad or gay she is no longer sad or gay. Always there is another self which is hidden from the mirror and which enables her to look at herself in the mirror. This other self tells her that it is only her image which is sad, only her image which is gay. By looking at herself steadily in the mirror she really accomplishes the miracle of not looking at herself. The mirror enables her to fall into a trance in which the image is completely lost. The eyes close and she falls backward into the deep. The whale too falls backward and is lost into the deep. (Miller 287-288)

The mirror mentioned here is quite different than the mirror in Jacques Lacan's "mirror stage." For Lacan, the mirror is any reflective surface (a mother's face, for example), in which a child recognizes his/her image and identifies with it (and the Other). The mirror which Miller imagines, however, does not involve a direct reflection or confrontation with the Self. It is, rather, the device which reflects the Other. Behind the mirror of the whale's bowels lies the world of the Other, but no one can break out of the whale. According to Miller, who was against psychoanalysis, one does not see the mirror of the Other to see oneself, but sees in the mirror of one's own consciousness the world of the Other.

Lacan's mirror stage presupposes the symmetry between the subject that sees and the object that is seen. And, as Luce Irigaray points out, the subject that sees and speaks has always been male, and the female is required to be the mirror/other/mother on which the male builds his ego. Irigaray denounces this notion of symmetry as a "phallocratic model": "As for the priority of symmetry, it co-relates with that of the flat mirror—which may be used for the self-reflection of the masculine subject in language, for its constitution as subject of discourse. Now woman, starting with this flat mirror alone, can only come into being as the inverted other of the masculine subject (his *alter ego*), or as the place of emergence and veiling of the cause of his (phallic) desire, or again as lack, since her sex for the most part—and the only historically valorized part—is not subject to specularization. Thus in the advent of a 'feminine' desire, this flat mirror cannot be privileged and symmetry cannot function as it does in the logic and discourse of a masculine subject" (Irigaray 129).

We should bring Jean Cocteau's *The Blood of a Poet* (1930) to mind, in which the protagonist is only able to enter into the mirror world "vertically." On the contrary, the protagonist in *Meshes of the Afternoon* never faces the mirror vertically. In Deren's works, the mirror is always slanted. The "dream girls" multiplied by repetition are never in accord with the self-portrait that might be reflected on the mirror when seen vertically. As shown in shot 112, they cast a languorous glance of the others, no matter how they look like each other.

The photographic works performed by Deren and shot by her husband Hammid quite often depend on the deforming effect of a mirror or glass. (Fig. 2) It looks as if Deren never puts confidence in what the mirror shows. According to the shooting script of *At Land*, the film was supposed to have a sequence which relied on mirrors, but the scenes were finally omitted.[3] In Sequence E, the protagonist enters a bedroom, which is found to be a multi-faceted mirror. The mirror multiplies her image to such a degree that the images are never face-to-face with each other, and the image that is seen does not meet the eye of the woman who sees. Although her face is reflected from different angles, she will never acquire the front image. (Fig. 3)

Fig. 2. From "Experimental Portraiture"

Fig. 3. An outtake from *At Land*

Now that we have seen how defiant Deren is of the symmetry of the mirror, it is no doubt that, for Deren, the mirror is not the device which reflects the Self, but the one that splits and multiplies the Self. Irigaray maintains that the revolt against the domination of the "flat mirror" over history "presupposes *a curved mirror*, but also one that is *folded back on itself*, with its impossible reappropriation 'on the inside' of the mind, of thought, of subjectivity" (Irigaray 155). This is exactly what Deren experimented on during the 1940s.

Let us return to the original question. Why does the destruction of the "mirror" cause the death of the Self? We have already reached the point where, because vertical symmetry is thoroughly challenged, the relation between question and answer is no longer considered as a one-to-one correspondence. We have also seen that Deren's mirror splits and multiplies. One possible answer to the question is: Even when she breaks the "mirror" in order to revolt against man, the very act of breaking the mirror reversely leads her to death as a woman, because in the real world it is always upon woman that society imposes the role of the mirror. Another answer is: At first she seems to have broken the "mirror" in order to repel the Other, but the destruction of the mirror only leads her to the destruction of her own mind because, as Henry Miller asserts, the mirror is something else than the Other, something which is attached inside and essential to the subject. All of these multiple interpretations we make are attributed to the traps that Deren elaborately set for us; a single, conclusive interpretation is impossible.

*Anaïs and Maya Before the Glass*

The shooting of *Rituals in Transfigured Time* started in August 1945. In Nin's diary, the first description of the shooting is in the entry of October 1945, in which she and her friends were asked to act in Deren's film. At first Nin's role was just to appear. Once the shooting started, however, Deren gave her "more and more to do," such as dancing (*Diary 4* 92).

While in *Meshes of the Afternoon* and *At Land* the girls who multiply are performed by Deren, she took a different approach in *Rituals in Transfigured Time*. This time the woman who splits is not performed by Deren alone, but played by multiple performers. Always interested in the sensuality of dancing, Deren designated Rita Christiani, a young dancer from Trinidad, as her double. In the original scenario, the roles of Deren and Christiani are interchangeable and signify the double aspects of one woman. The original scenario did not have the slightest mention of Nin's role (Clark 472). The role of another woman played by Nin was added as the shooting went on.

When their friendship began in 1944, Nin appreciated Deren's talent and vitality for filmmaking, admitting that Deren is "stronger than I am" (*Diary 4* 90) and described Deren's beauty in a scene from *Meshes of the Afternoon* as "a truly Botticelli effect" (76). Once she joined the filmmaking, however, Nin found Deren's strength to be merely the arbitrary power of the director. The shooting went on until the next year, and, in the entries of March and May of 1946, Nin harshly criticized Deren's work in progress.

There is no doubt that Nin and Deren had mutual sympathy for their common theme of woman's subjectivity, no matter what creative media they used. In April 1946, Nin wrote in her diary:

> All the various women may converge into one because down deep, in the unconscious, there are resemblances.
>
> Also in life women become other women, interchange, identify, and project. Parts of themselves in the other, through the other. There are exchanges, interchanges, and convergences, and parts of ourselves pass into others. (140)

It is quite probable that Nin wrote this passage under the influence of Deren, as we can find the word "interchange" in Deren's original scenario called "Ritual and Ordeal." While Nin truly understood that the theme of the film was interchangeabilty, she determined that the theme was lost and the film was a failure (149).

*Rituals in Transfigured Time* has a party scene in which several of Nin's friends appear. Rita strays into the party room. After the repetitive exchanges of useless greetings, Rita finally meets the man of fate, played by the dancer Frank Westbrook. Then the scene changes suddenly from interior to exterior. In the exterior scene, men and women dance, and Rita has ambivalent emotions towards Frank, such as fear and yearning, and runs away. She runs and runs from Frank until she reaches the museum court, where she finds Frank frozen as a statue. She is extremely frightened and runs again. Maya takes over the running and does not hesitate to dive into the water. The protagonist switches to Rita diving underwater, and the screen image is inverted into the negative. The negative close-up of Rita's face from the last scene refuses to give us any clue to a single, fixed meaning (Fig. 4). Is it fear and agony, or peace and relief that she expresses? In terms of an inverted image, this close-up also has a mirror effect. In the works of Maya Deren, the mirror always subverts and displaces the meaning.

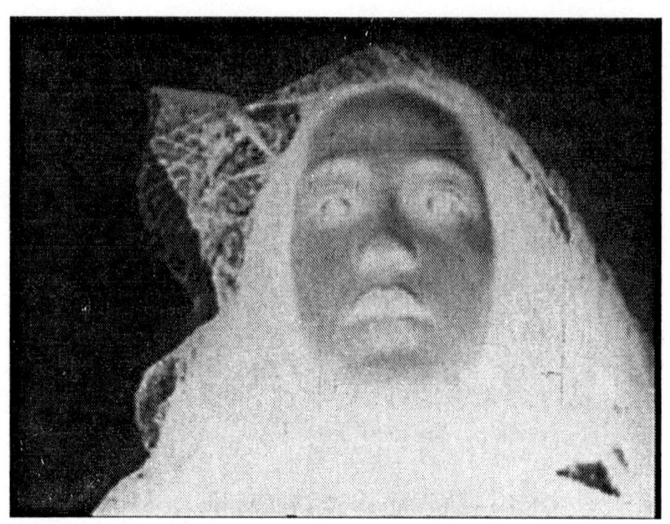

Fig. 4. The last shot of *Rituals in Transfigured Time*

To criticize *Rituals in Transfigured Time*, Nin used the word "empty" or "emptiness" several times. After the twelve hours of filming the party scene, Nin was exhausted, realizing that what they had acted out was emptiness (*Diary 4* 135-136). This criticism sounds strange because it is quite obvious that the aim of this prolonged scene in the 15-minute short film is to visualize emptiness. What really irritated Nin was presumably her feeling that she was treated like a pawn for Maya's caricature. Furthermore, Nin denounced the film for having "no sensual connection" between the men and women (136). Most of the cast are, according to Nin, homosexuals. This again is a strange attack, for, as is pointed out, the film was apparently intended to question heterosexuality (Pramaggiore 252).

We can presume that Deren and Nin had heated discussions, but most of the surviving material is written exclusively by Nin. One of the few things that Deren left behind is a poem dedicated to Nin. Written in August, 1945, when the shooting had just started, the poem sounds like a predictive objection to the criticism Nin would make the next year:

> For Anaïs Before the Glass
> By Maya Deren
>
> The mirror, like a cannibal, consumed,
> carnivorous, blood-silvered, all the life fed it.
> You too have known this merciless transfusion
> along the arm by which we each have held it.

In the illusion was pursued the vision
through the reflection to the revelation.
The miracle has come to pass.
Your pale face, Anaïs, before the glass
at last is not returned to you reversed.

This is no longer mirrors, but an open wound
through which we face each other framed in blood.

August 19, 1945 (Clark 537)

Once you stand before the mirror, you have to resign yourself to the carnivorous consumption. These sound like overly audacious words to address the writer, fourteen years older. It can be read as a declaration requiring self-sacrifice to the artwork. Nin's pale face is not simply returned to her as a reversed image. For Deren, to stand before the mirror is to look into an open wound and see the bloody figure. Always facing her mirror-diary, Nin should have recognized "this merciless transfusion."

Nin and her friends, however, completely changed their attitude towards Deren, according to the diary entry of May, 1946. It was Nin who had introduced her to Frank Westbrook, who played the important role of driving Rita, the protagonist, to change. According to the diary, Nin became more nervous than Westbrook himself when Deren required him to leap from one rock to another in naked feet. Westbrook did jump, but the filmed footage was found to be unsatisfying to Deren, so that the scene was finally cut. This kind of perfectionism seemed inhuman to Nin (*Diary 4* 146-147).

The day she saw the finished film, Nin became filled with anger. She had confessed previously that she was the oldest and feared close-ups, but Hammid had assured her that the editing would respect her concerns. Seeing herself in the finished film, however, Nin was quite shocked to find that her close-up (Fig. 5) was "shiny-skinned and distorted by magnification," while Deren had always been made beautiful by the editing (156). It is more likely that Nin was discontented with Deren's arbitrariness than with her lines of age revealed, for some thought "Maya made Anaïs look quite wonderful" (Fitch 279).

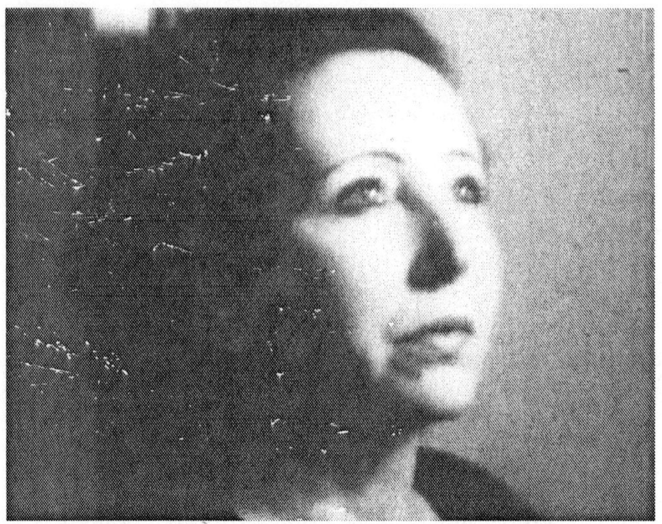

Fig. 5. Anaïs Nin in *Rituals in Transfigured Time*

"The camera can be a lover, or a hater, or a sadist, or a defamer... It lies" (*Diary 4* 351). Nin went on: "The quest for ugliness is one I never understood. Was it because Americans were for the most part born in ugliness, familiar with it, and had grown to love it, or because they associated beauty with the undemocratic upper class, art, the past, Europe, and repudiated it? The American definition of realism was ugliness. To avoid being accused of creating illusion, they always showed the same ugly view of everything. Maya magnified the skin blemishes, the knotted nerves, the large ears; she stressed the oily surfaces, the thyroid white of the eyes, the baldness or the pimple. Maya's actors happened to be beautiful. She uglified them. I had never seen as clearly as in Maya, the power to uglify in the eye behind the camera" (353).

This kind of challenge to American naturalist realism is quite familiar to the readers of Anaïs Nin. We remember, for example, how conflicted Nin was with Henry Miller's grotesque portrayal of Paris during the 1930s, how his wife June resented being portrayed as ugly in his writings. Nin asked him why he wrote more about June's defects and less about her magnificence. The answer is: "...I take goodness for granted. I expect everybody to be good. It is evil which fascinates me" (*Henry and June* 135).

Involving her friends with her filmmaking, paying no fees or transportation costs, and, according to Nin, concentrating on her filmmaking so inhumanly, Deren could be compared with Miller, who, in the 1930s, wrote *Tropic of Cancer* and other writings while living off his friends. In the climax scene of *Henry and June*, where June accuses Miller of making a monster out of her by distortion, Nin shows her sympathy for both of them: "I am not vacillating between Henry and June, between their contradictory versions of themselves, but between two truths I see with clarity. I believe in Henry's humanness, although I am fully aware of the literary monster. I believe in June, although I am aware of her innocent destructive power and her comedies" (270-1).

Her diary tells us how, in the chaos of her muses Henry and June, Nin developed into a writer, which seems to imply that she should also have understood Maya was a filmmaking "monster." *The Diary of Anaïs Nin, Volume 4* came out in 1971, when Deren was already gone. The "feud" between them was, therefore, a story which was concocted long after Deren's passing. In 1975, when asked about Deren ignoring the promises to not to use close-ups, Nin answered: "[T]oday I wouldn't blame her for that. Because I've watched films being made. And I realize that the film was more important than ourselves. We just wanted to see ourselves a certain way. We were not professional" (*A Woman Speaks* 254). In spite of this realization, Nin published her diary, written thirty years previously, without apparent modification, which shows that Nin herself was possibly a literary "monster."

Concerning the quarrel between the two artists, Ute Holl gives us the following observation: Whereas Nin trusts in the mirror as a registering device, Deren believes in the mirror as a highly creative instrument (Holl 153). This picture is quite useful, but their relationship seems more complicated. To read the story of their "feud," we can depend only on Nin's diary.[4] This is the trap that the diary, "the document of the truth," sets for us. Whereas Nin's diary account is that she was made ugly by Deren's filmmaking, the same charge could be made in reverse: that it was Deren who was made ugly in the diary. Although Nin presented Deren as a "monster" in her diary, the fact is that Nin truly appreciated Deren's talent. And perhaps Deren, who wrote "Your pale face, Anaïs, before the glass / at last is not returned to you reversed," would accept that her face was not simply returned to her from the mirror of Nin's diary. Their mirrors were indeed the ones through which they faced each other "framed in blood."

We cannot be accept simply that Nin expressed anger for Deren in her diary, because is it not possible she was trying to honestly expose her own immature feelings, one of which is anger? It was very daring for a female writer to express anger in 1971, let alone 1946, because, in a male-centric society, in which the woman's role is supposed to be "mirror-mother," her anger is not expected. Anger was a privileged territory for male writers. Deviation from the role of "mirror-mother" is where Nin and Deren come together. For the two artists, to stand before the mirror is to revolt against the traditional domination of the "flat mirror," the "vertical" domination of the subject who oversees the object whom is seen. Anaïs before Maya, Maya before Anaïs, standing before the curved mirror, the two women split, multiply, interchange, and finally converge into one. In doing so, they became accomplices—that is, being woman—in the revolt against the traditional subject of discourse. ◈

## *Works Cited*


*DVDs*

*Maya Deren: Experimental Films*. New York: Mystic Fire Video, 2002.

*In the Mirror of Maya Deren*. Dir. Martina Kudlácek. New York: Zeitgeist Films, 2004.

*Books*

Clark, VèVè A., Millicent Hodson and Catrina Neiman, eds. *The Legend of Maya Deren: A Documentary Biography and Collected Works, vol. I, pt. II: Chambers (1942-1947)*. New York: Anthology Film Archives, 1988.

Deren, Maya. "Amateur versus Professional." *Essential Deren: Collected Writings on Film*. Ed. Bruce R. McPherson. Kingston, New York: Documentext, 2005.

Fitch, Noël Riley. *Anaïs: The Erotic Life of Anaïs Nin*. Boston: Little, Brown, 1993.

Holl, Ute. "Moving the Dancers' Souls." *Maya Deren and the American Avant-Garde*. Ed. Bill Nichols. Los Angeles: University of California Press, 2001.

Irigaray, Luce. *This Sex Which Is Not One*. Trans. Catherine Porter and Caroline Burke. Ithaca, NY: Cornell University Press, 1985.

Miller Henry. "Un Être Étoilique." *The Cosmological Eye*. New York: New Directions, 1939.

Nin, Anaïs. *The Diary of Anaïs Nin, Vol. 1, 1931-1934*. Ed. Gunther Stuhlmann. New York: Harcourt Brace Jovanovich, 1966.

----. *The Diary of Anaïs Nin, Vol. 4, 1944-1947*. Ed. Gunther Stuhlmann. New York: Harcourt Brace Jovanovich, 1971.

----. *The Diary of Anaïs Nin, Vol. 6, 1955-1966*. Ed. Gunther Stuhlmann. New York: Harcourt Brace Jovanovich, 1977.

----. *Henry and June*. New York: Harcourt Brace Jovanovich, 1986.

----. *A Woman Speaks: The Lectures, Seminars and Interviews of Anaïs Nin.* Ed. Evelyn Hinz. Athens, Ohio: Swallow Press, 1975.

Pramaggiore, Maria. "Seeing Double(s): Reading Deren Bisexually." *Maya Deren and the American Avant-Garde.* Ed. Bill Nichols. Los Angeles: University of California Press, 2001.

Sontag, Susan. *Against Interpretation and Other Essays.* New York: Picador, 2001.

*Notes*

---

[1] Anaïs Nin noted in her diary "[t]wo men" (*Diary 4* 75). Actually, those who were shooting were Alexander Hammid and a female assistant Hella Heyman. After Deren and Hammid divorced, he married Heyman.

[2] In Martina Kudlácek's documentary film *In the Mirror of Maya Deren,* Marcia Vogel, a co-director of Cinema 16 Film Society, where the films of Maya Deren were screened, speaks of Deren: "She [Maya] was just a woman ahead of her time… So à la the '60s, with flower children and stuff."

[3] Clark 181. Published in 1988, the book is annotated, saying sequence E was "never filmed" (175). Later, the footage was found and the outtake is fragmentarily inserted into *In the Mirror of Maya Deren.*

[4] In the interview in 1975, Maya's ex-husband Hammid reemphasized the feud between Nin and Deren, saying "She [Anaïs] hates me and Maya because we didn't make her beautiful in the film" (Clark 538). On the other hand, Noël Riley Fitch writes in her biography of Nin: "Contrary to the impression left by the diary, Nin and Deren remain outwardly friendly… In the mid-1950s Anaïs and Maya are even planning film together about labyrinths, using Wall Street as a setting" (Fitch 342).

*Joel Enos*

## Anaïs Nin's "Incest Family"

*The distraction of loving the self in others*

Gary Sayre writes in his essay "*House of Incest*: Two Interpretations" about the differences between the traditional Freudian definition of the word "incest" and Anaïs Nin's use of it as a symbolic literary tool:

> *Incest* is a word that most commonly evokes the image of a mother/son, father/daughter, and/or brother/sister relationship or act which is primarily sexual. In Freud's psychosexual theory of personality development every child experiences early in life a sexual desire for his mother or father. However incest is not really a symbol at all in the Freudian view, for a symbol in this view stands only for that which the ego cannot in reality possess; therefore, the ego creates images of the thing it wants to possess, i.e., a symbol has only as much meaning as the ego assigns to it...in an overstated way, then, *House of Incest* must express a symbolic significance deeper than the common Freudian view can penetrate, or even begin to illuminate...incest symbolizes or should I say signifies any form of self-love which is essentially selfish, or ego-oriented. It is a love which seeks only to possess the "other" and only inasmuch as this possession be a reflection of itself: "If only we could all escape from this house of incest, where we only love ourselves in the other." (Sayre 46-7)

Anaïs Nin's narcissistic incest occurs when people look for their ideal selves in other people. It is a "self-defeating and narcissistic love" (Fitch 132). Instead of loving another person, the incest-afflicted character loves him/herself within that person. In *House of Incest*, Sabina's "love is a lie; she doesn't love anyone but herself. It is a self-love which can only exist by consuming others, a desire which is insatiable. She is the female version of Don Juan" (Sayre 47). In extreme cases, the cycle of what I call the "incest family" brings people to create an environment of doubles, a house of incest:

> Many people invent situations, invent each other, to satisfy some obscure psychological need. These imaginary relationships, acted in a void, not only may take a great deal of our energies, but are doomed to frustration. (*Novel of the Future* 77)

Once the incestuous qualities inherent in this form of projection are realized, the afflicted can better deal with them. Nin's literature offers multiple examples of doubling, the futility of acting in the void of the incest family and the final realization that one must stop the cycle of incest, looking within rather than without, to find the self.

In Nin's first novel, *House of Incest*, the unnamed female narrator encounters characters locked in various forms of self love. The narrator herself becomes afflicted with incest when she meets Sabina: "Sabina and the writer of the poem are in constant danger of identifying with each other and *becoming the other*" (*Novel of the Future* 122-3). The narrator tells Sabina: "When I saw you, Sabina, I chose my body... I AM THE OTHER FACE OF YOU... THIS IS THE BOOK YOU WROTE AND YOU ARE THE WOMAN I AM" (*House of Incest* 27-8). Because another character, Jeanne, is in love with her brother, she satisfies "the conventional Freudian expectation" (Sayre 48), but the incest bond between them symbolizes something more:

> The essence of Jeanne's self-love...contains spiritual significance beyond the superficial interpretation that her neurosis or "madness" consists merely of her perverted desire for a sexual relationship with her brother... Her brother is an idealized image of herself, a subjectively created self-image she cannot "find" because it is without substance, without body; it is self-illusion. (Sayre 48)

Sayre's theory rests on the fact that when Jeanne finally finds her brother in the house of incest, she can only touch his shadow:

> When my brother sat in the sun and his face was shadowed on the back of the chair I kissed his shadow. I kissed his shadow and this kiss did not touch him, this kiss was lost in the air and melted with the shadow. Our love of each other is like one long shadow kissing, without hope of reality. (*House of Incest* 48)

This love has no hope of reality because Jeanne and her brother are shadows of each other, doubles. They love themselves. This twinship is foreshadowed when we first encounter Jeanne:

> She sang and she laughed: I love my brother.
>
> I love my brother. I want crusades and martyrdom. I find the world too small.
>
> Salted tears of defeat crystallized in the corners of her restless eyes.
>
> But I never weep.

> She picked up a mirror and looked at herself with love.
> Narcisse gazing at himself in Lanvin mirrors. (44)

In one instance, Jeanne is loving both her brother and her self in the mirror. Jeanne leads us and the narrator into the house of incest. Symbolizing the stagnancy of loving the self in others, moments of arrest fill the house of incest distracting Jeanne from her journey toward the self, leaving her with no sense of direction:

> Everything had been made to stand still in the house of incest, because they all had such a fear of movement and warmth, such a fear that all love and all life should flow out of reach and be lost. Everything had been made to stand still, and everything was rotting away… Standing still for many years, between the moment she had lost her brother and the moment she had looked at the facade of the house of incest, moving in endless circles round the corners of the dreams, never reaching the end of her voyage... (52, 61)

In addition, when she finds her brother, he tells her that he is enamored, not with her, but her portrait:

> Jeanne, I fell asleep among the paintings, where I could sit for many days worshipping your portrait. I fell in love with your portrait, Jeanne, because it will never change. I have such a fear of seeing you grow old, Jeanne; I fell in love with an unchanging you that will never be taken away from me. I was wishing you would die, so that no one could ever take you away from me, and I would love the painting of you as you would look eternally. They bowed to one part of themselves only—their likeness. (61)

He wishes her to remain arrested in time. Being her double, he is in love with his own portrait and wishes himself to remain frozen in time, to die.

Pierre's confusion in "Je Suis Le Plus Malade Des Surrealistes" is similar to Jeanne's brother's narcissistic affliction with her (his) portrait. Pierre's sister tells him:

> "Brother, brother...you are confusing the nature of our love for each other... Brother, brother... I have such a deep love for you, but do not touch me. I am not to be touched. You are the poet, you walk inside my dreams. I love the pain and the flame in you, but do not touch me." (*Under a Glass Bell* 52, 54)

Touching her, loving her, would be the ultimate distraction from accepting himself and her for who they actually are. Loving his sister would constitute loving the physical embodiment of his psychological double.[1]

The dangers of loving the double are explained to Jean in "The All-Seeing":

> "People who are twins," I said, "there is a curse upon their love. Love is made of differences and suffering and apartness, and of the struggle to overcome this apartness. Two people who love the dream above all else would soon both vanish together. One of them must be on the earth to hold the other down. And the pain of being held down by the earth, reality, that is what our love for "others will be." (*Under a Glass Bell* 75-6)

Jean responds by saying, "I see myself free when I look at you," ignoring the narrator's warning, loving the free self in the narrator. Confused by the mixed-up affection present in the house of incest, the narrator of *House of Incest* subsequently becomes lost within the pages of the book:

> I walked into my own book, seeking peace. It was night, and I made a careless move inside the dream; I turned too brusquely the corner and I bruised myself against my madness... I carry white sponges of knowledge on strings of nerves. As I move within my book I am cut by pointed glass and broken bottles in which there is still the odor of sperm and perfume. (*House of Incest* 62)

The multiple doubling of Jeanne, her brother, the portrait of Jeanne, Sabina and the Modern Christ, an enigmatic character appearing in the last sections of *House*, have left her directionless and lost in the house of incest.

Robert Rogers, in *A Psychoanalytic Study of the Double in Literature*, distinguishes between the many types of doubling involved in literature as a whole. Anaïs Nin's doubles occur when people project feelings of close kinship or camaraderie onto another person in the hopes that, through that twin or double, they will be able to locate themselves. Rather than look inward, they wish to observe someone else to find the key to their own inner self. Doubling, then, is essentially creating a twin out of someone else to find one's own self within them. In the case of literary doubling, the double becomes another character in the story, symbolizing the narcissistic projection that may occur in waking life: "Narcissism paradoxically involves a relationship, a relationship of self to self in which one's self is regarded as though it were another person" (Rogers 18).

Nin's writing is flooded with images of the double. Many of her characters seek out people who share a common philosophy or fear. Most of them are escaping from an all-controlling father. By grouping together with each other, they attempt to keep the father out of their midst. I call this incest world that a person creates out of doubles the "incest family." The fatherless incest family that Nin's characters create in her fiction eradicates the all-controlling father by placing the daughter at the helm of the incest family in the role of the all-controlling mother figure. The daughter in the novella "Winter of Artifice" epitomizes the recurring wish among Nin's characters to be free of the father:

> To escape him she had run away to the end of the world. To be free of him she had run away to places where he never went. She had lost him, by living in the opposite direction from him. No trace of him anywhere along the boulevard Clichy where the market people passed with their little vegetable carts; no trace of him at two in the morning in the little café opposite La Trinité; no trace of him in the sordid neighborhood of the Boulevard Jean-Jaurès; no trace of him in the *cinema quartier*, in the Bal Musette, in the burlesque theatre. Never anyone who had heard of him. Never anyone who smelled like him. Never a voice like his. (*Winter of Artifice* 73)

Djuna in *Children of the Albatross* also strives to be rid of the father: "In Djuna the wound had remained alive, and whenever life touched upon this wound she mistook the pain for being alive, and her pain warning her and guiding her to deflect from man the father to man the son" (*Cities of the Interior* 196). Both characters construct an incest family out of grown children: "There are plenty of children, abandoned children right in the so-called grown-ups" (35). The members of the daughter's and Djuna's respective incest families harbor the same rebellious disregard for a traditional father.

Often in Nin's work, a father figure will appear who makes contact between doubles and incest families difficult or impossible. She will use the interference of an authority figure in several of her later works of fiction. Noel Riley Fitch writes that the novels in which these authority figures appear

> reflect several tensions of [Anaïs Nin's] adolescent fears: the feeling of abandonment—her protagonists are frequently orphans; the abuse

> and authority of an older male figure...and being kept from intimacy with a youthful (often homosexual) male twin. (Fitch 40-1)

The father figure in Djuna's childhood is the lecherous night watchman at the orphanage where she grew up who "lifted the corners of our bedcovers, and let his eyes rove and sometimes more than his eyes..." (*Cities of the Interior* 26-7). He would make her "be good" to him before he would allow her to leave and meet her boyfriend. His activities help steer her from the father-man to the son-man, the child:

> The way the watchman stood, demanded, gestured, was all part of a will she did not even question, a continuation of the will of the father. There was the man who demanded, and outside was the gentle boy who demanded nothing, and to whom she wanted to give everything, whose silence even, she trusted, whose way of walking she trusted with her entire heart, while this man she did not trust. (140)

The person she does trust is Michael, a gentle boy, who does not demand anything of Djuna because he is gay. She falls into a cycle of being forever attracted to "other Michaels in the world":

> Some part of her continued to recognize the same gentleness, the same elusiveness, the same mystery... But the same little dance took place each time, a little dance of insolence, a dance which said to the woman: "I dance alone, I will not be possessed by a woman." (155)

Paradoxically, because she wants a non-controlling man in her life, she is drawn to men who do not want to possess her in a sexual way. But, she confuses their lack of attraction to women with immaturity and is drawn to this immaturity because such a man cannot be a father-figure to her.

Djuna's affair with the adolescent, Paul, brings her into opposition with his parents and especially his controlling father. Paul is a "prisoner," "the son of tyrannical parents" who send a detective to bring him home when he runs away. Eventually, Paul moves into her house and accepts her care. She takes on the role of mother to him as well as teacher and first lover. For a while, their union acts as a barrier to the father, just as an all-woman barrier would: "Once there they both felt secure from all the world, and from all threats, from the father and the detective, and all the taboos erected to separate lovers all over the world" (184). Aside from Paul's controlling father, the other male characters in *Albatross*, almost exclusively homosexual, take to Paul in a brotherly way that never usurps Djuna's place as the head of the incest household.

Near the end of their relationship in *Children of the Albatross*, we can see Paul himself changing into someone who may threaten Djuna's matriarchal role:

> How dare the father command now! Doesn't he hear the new voice of the new man in his son?
>
> He hung up.
>
> His hair was falling over his eager eyes. Djuna pulled at it. He stopped her. "You can't do that anymore, oh no." And he sank his teeth into the softest part of her neck. (183)

He is beginning to assert himself as the controller in the relationship, but the relationship ends when Paul's father asserts his "restrictive severity" and takes him home. In a sense, even the father is still under the control of his own father, further demonstrating the strength and emphasis placed on the role of fatherhood.

A liaison between members of the incest family breaches certain familial boundaries, just as familial incest does in its traditional setting:

> [Miguel] suffered at times more than the women, whose vanity was all that mattered. He had such a familial relationship with women, that he always felt as if he were wounding a mother, sister, or Elena again, in her new transformations. (*Delta of Venus* 172)

When a woman tries to seduce a homosexual male, she puts him in a position where he has no choice but to take some sort of control of the situation. Similarly, when the female in "Our Minds are Engaged," a short story in *Waste of Timelessness*, seduces the male into a relationship, he starts trying to change her and becomes father-like:

> He said: "I want you to be more real with me." He did not mean more real but more subject to his own evaluations... Unexpectedly, she realized his tyranny was not that of a lover but of one who cannot love. She realized he wanted to make himself feel strong by making her weaker. (*Waste of Timelessnes* 55-6)

Being homosexual, he cannot return her love the way she wants him to. To hide his self-resentment and shame at his inability to love her, he changes into a tyrannical version of a father figure, destroying their feeling of twinship that initially brought them together.

Homosexuals and rebels make easy doubles for women to incorporate as children into their incest families for such figures pit themselves against the traditional father as much as she does. The psychoanalytic view of homosexuality during the time Anaïs Nin was writing was that it was a form of immaturity. In Nin's literature, homosexuality is likened to femininity and childishness. The homosexual man in "Our Minds are Engaged" is drawn to men, "yet conscious of the immaturity, the incompleteness" (*Waste of Timelessness* 47) of his instinct. Homosexuality can also be linked to narcissism. Narcissism of this sort fits nicely into Nin's scheme of incest. In the erotic story "Elena," Miguel is frightened by what he sees his brothers doing with whores: "What was there left for Miguel to turn to with his desires? Boys, boys without the gluttonous openings, boys with sexes like his, that did not frighten him, whose desires he could satisfy" (*Delta of Venus* 112). The term "boy" likens Miguel's homosexuality to a childish fear of adult sexuality.

Though she sees Miguel's lover Donald as a child, Elena finds a double in him:

> Miguel, in need of someone other than his analyst to confide in, introduced Elena to his lover, Donald. As soon as Elena saw Donald she loved him too, as she would a child, an *enfant terrible,* perverse and knowing... When Miguel left them at the café table for a moment, they looked at each other with a stare of recognition. Without Miguel, Donald was no longer a woman. He straightened his body, looked at her unflinchingly, and talked about how he was seeking intensity and tension saying that Miguel was not the father he needed—Miguel was too young, Miguel was just another child. (114-5)

Donald is a male version of Elena. He complains to her of his sexual inequality with Miguel, yet when she witnesses a sexual act between them, she realizes that he appropriates the submissive role willingly. When Elena witnesses the two men having sex, she identifies with Donald, her double: "The scene in the dark affected her strangely. She felt part of herself sharing in it, as a woman, she as a woman within Donald's boy body, being made love to by Miguel" (119). At the same time, Elena is reading her own lover's, Pierre's, letter proclaiming his love to her. She leaves to meet Pierre, who hurt her years before by abruptly leaving her, to give herself to him, as her male double is giving himself to Donald. Donald seems no more capable of changing his role than she is capable of changing hers.

In Nin's work, the connection between women and gay men in the incest family hinges on their defiant adolescent-like rebelliousness. She explains this in an interview with Karla Jay from *Everywoman* magazine in 1971:

> [Karla Jay]: Sometimes I sensed in your diary a great deal of ambiguity in your relationship to homosexual men. On the one hand, as you say, you felt they were childish and immature, but you seem to see another side to them—which was a rebellion against society and against the man-woman relationship.
>
> [Anaïs Nin]: Which I shared with them, yes... Yes, a kinship with the rebels. Of course I can't bring things into the present, but in the past, you see, Henry Miller was a rebel against Puritanism, Otto Rank was a rebel against Freudianism, Antonin Artaud was a rebel against surrealism, and I was always allied to the rebels... I've always been with the one who rebels against false values... They were not all homosexual. They were very sensitive, and they were very young and against the establishment. They seemed much more open and much more alive... I call them the transparent children and it just happened by coincidence that most of them were homosexual. When you welcomed them, of course, you had to get caught in a circle because they do move in a sort of fraternal group. So I happened to have met them all at that time and they were much more interesting to me than the other people I compared them to—the mature writers. (Dubow, 139; 138)

For Nin, gay and childlike men are perpetual sons. With them, women can create an incest family of doubles without bringing in a father. However, a narcissistic person searching for the self in doubles, loving the self in others, is at risk of falling in love with the double. Elena's attraction to Miguel mirrors Djuna's to Michael in *Children of the Albatross*.[2] This attraction to the perpetual son is also played out in "Our Minds are Engaged." The female character feels that the homosexual she pursues simply needs a woman to set him straight: "He was in destructive conflict. What he desired was wholeness and normalcy, through the love of woman. To be made to feel whole, entire, man" (*Children of the Albatross* 46). Djuna wonders in *Children*: "When will I stop loving these airy young men." (160).

Later, Elena confuses love of "airy young men" with a desire to be like them:

> Elena was laughing. She was thinking that when Pierre turned his back to her, he became like a woman for her, and she would have

> liked to rape him. She could well imagine Miguel's feelings when he lay against Donald's back. (*Delta of Venus* 171)

Elena imagines what she thinks Miguel must feel for Donald, but she does not want to be a gay man. However, in her confused state, she seems to want to be Miguel. She is not yet able to recognize that the closeness she feels to him is mainly due to her recognizing bits of her own self in his actions. She seems to subconsciously feel that she must emulate him to understand him, a process which will then lead her closer to understanding herself. The fact that she is identifying with a man is confusing because she is not one and cannot possibly understand how Michael would actually feel as he "lay against Donald's back."

But, when the double is another woman, not a gay man, the same sort of confusion arises. When Sabina and Lillian have a sexual encounter in *Ladders to Fire*, both react by deciding that a sexual relationship is not what they are looking for:

> They separated and saw it was not this they wanted, sought, dreamed. Not this possession they imagined. No bodies touching would ever answer this mysterious craving in them to become each other. Not to possess each other but to become each other. Not to take, but to imbibe, absorb, change themselves. (104)

Like Elena, the women are trying to find themselves by changing into someone else, trying to look at themselves through someone else's eyes. They do not love each other so much as they love their own selves, or their pictures of their respective ideal selves, within the other.[3] Lillian tells Sabina: "I have a feeling that I want to be you, Sabina. I never wanted to be anyone but myself before" (95).

Lillian's confusion is dissipated later, in *Seduction of the Minotaur*, when she finally comes to understand her desire for Sabina:

> It was a desire for an impossible union: she wanted to lose herself in Sabina and BECOME Sabina. This wanting to BE Sabina she had mistaken for love of Sabina's night beauty. She wanted to lie beside her and become her and be one with her and both arise as ONE woman; she wanted to add herself to Sabina, re-enforce the woman in herself, the submerged woman, intensify this woman Lillian she could not liberate fully. (578-9)

Similarly, in *Ladders to Fire*, Djuna finds Lillian imitating her: "She wants something of me that only a man can give her. But first of all she wants to become me, so that she can communicate with man"

(37). Similarly, in "Elena," after Elena has confided in Miguel about her sexual relationship with Leila and Mary, he tells her: "That's not such a great infidelity, Elena. In another woman you're only seeking yourself" (*Delta of Venus* 145). In her essay, "Library of the Ultravixens," Elizabeth Young examined a similar encounter in Mary Gaitskill's novel *Two Girls, Fat and Thin*:

> The two girls end up in bed together...and the two halves of what might be read as one personality are reconciled. Justine welcomes the rejected outsider in herself and Dorothy receives the validation of her intellectual self. Together they form an impregnable female unity against the misbegotten power of all sadistic fathers. (Young, 180)

In Gaitskill's novel, homosexuality, as well as doubling, is a method of keeping the controlling father away. Similarly, when Sabina and Lillian are falling in love, Nin writes: "We hate Jay tonight. We hate man" (*Cities of the Interior* 99). Oddly, taking the man or father out of their relationship, the women become confused, appropriating the missing aspects of masculinity themselves to defend their man-less union.

In the novella "The Voice,"[4] the character, the Voice, represents the purely psychoanalytic point of view, although later he seems to find fault with his own method and practice,[5] and notes masculine characteristics that Lillian has appropriated to make herself not weak like a woman, but strong like a man:

> In each gesture a swing intended to be masculine, but as soon as she sat on the couch, looking up at the Voice, flushed with timidity, saying: "shall I take off my shoes and lie down," he knew already that she was not masculine. She was deluding herself and others about it. (*Winter of Artifice* 91)

Lillian's seductions of Hazel and Georgia are interpreted by the Voice as Lillian trying to be strong or masculine by being like a man. When another patient, Lilith,[6] tells the Voice that she no longer needs a father, he says: "I am not entirely sure that the little girl in you ever died, or her need of a father. What am I to you?" (109). Later in the story, Djuna and Lilith have a sexual encounter similar to that of Lillian and Sabina's in *Ladders to Fire*. Once again, Nin emphasizes that the two are doubles of each other:

> "But none of this is love, Lilith. We are the same woman.[7] There is always the moment when all the outlines, the differences between women disappear...we lose our separate identities. What happens to

> you is the same as what happens to me. Listening to you is not entering a world different from my own, it's a kind of communion." (*Cities of the Interior* 119)

Their sexual encounter is described as a "twinship." Nin's women always seem to come to the conclusion that the closeness they desired is not found in sexuality but an unattainable twinship that they believe they can somehow find in a double.[8] Lilith progresses further than Lillian by the end of the story. Mirroring Sabina in the end of *A Spy in the House of Love*, she leaves Djuna, the double, and returns to the Voice, the helping hand of therapy. Djuna, unassisted by a guide or therapist, continues to struggle with the dream of the land-locked boat:

> *With the night came the boat. This boat I was pushing with all my strength because it could not float, it was passing through land. It was chokingly struggling along the streets, it could not find its way to the ocean. It was pushed along the streets of the city, touching the walls of houses, and I was pushing against the resistance of the earth.* (*Winter of Artifice* 129)

Her narcissistic attraction to Lilith leaves her stranded, burdened as Sabina whose Don Juanesque escapades leave her fragmented:

> Sabina was no longer embracing men and women. Within the fever of her restlessness the world was losing its human shape. She was losing the power to fit body to body in human completeness. She was delimiting the horizons, sinking into the planets without axis, losing her polarity and the divine knowledge of integration, of fusion. (*House of Incest* 24-5)

For Sabina, the incessant and continuous pattern of having multiple lovers leaves her feeling out of control, unaware, even, of what she is actually looking for in those lovers.

Otto Rank's theory of the Don Juan complex is based on the traditional premise of Don Juan looking for love and sex but being unable to find them together in one lover. Nin's own theory of Don Juanism adds a dimension to Rank's: A Don Juan is not merely searching for love and sex; he's searching for himself through his many lovers:

> "Oh, no. Don Juan was seeking in passion, in the act of possession, in the welding of bodies, something that has nothing to do with passion and was never born of it."

> "A Narcissus pool," Jay said.
>
> "No, he was seeking to be created, to be born, to be warmed into existence, to be known, to be identified, he was seeking a proactive miracle..." ("Sabina" 35)

This passage exhibits Nin's concordance with Rank, who felt that a Don Juan daughter, seducing women, is attempting to recreate the activity of the father to find her self.

The novella "Winter of Artifice," formerly titled both "Father Story" and "The Double," deals directly with a Don Juan daughter overcoming a Don Juan father. In it, prompted by her father's inability to remain faithful to her mother, a daughter reunites with her father after a twenty year separation. Upon reacquaintance, they discover themselves in each other and begin to participate in a narcissistic love. Because of her father's abandonment of her family when she was a child, the daughter is chronically sensitive and insecure:

> She was a perpetually offended being who fancied that she was not wanted... The smallest incident could arouse an anguish as great as that caused by death, and could reawaken the pain of separation as keenly as she had experienced it the day her father had gone away. (*Winter of Artifice* 45, 50)

To find herself she feels that she must recognize her resemblance to him. One major similarity between them is that the daughter's love life is as scattered as her Don Juan father's. Her insecurity drives her to men who resemble him:

> Having been so faithful to his image as she had been, having loved his image in other men, having been moved by the men who played the piano, the men who talked brilliantly, intellectuals, teachers, philosophers, doctors, every man with blue eyes, every man with an adventurous life, every Don Juan… (52)

The actual man she wishes to seduce, to prove she is worthy, is the one who originally left her, her father.

Yet, when he arrives, the father is described as "feminine" and "youthful," not "at all like a father." These terms color him as a double of the young woman, but he maintains the role of the controlling father. The doubles are not equal:

> "You are my daughter. We think the same. We laugh at the same things. You owe me nothing. You have created yourself alone, but I gave you the seed."
>
> ...In the world she made alone she was lonely. She, being a woman, had to live in a manmade world, could not impose her own, but here was her father's world, it fitted her... He thought and felt the same thing at the same time...
>
> "I never knew a woman I could take into my world." (49)

Risking losing herself in her father's world, the daughter finally gets close enough to him to find the differences between them:

> The difference is this, she begins to see, that he wears gloves for gardening and so does she, but he is afraid of poverty, and she is not. Can she prove that? *Must* she prove that? Why? For herself. She must know wherein she is not like him. She must disentangle their two selves. (65)

These differences are what will finally set her free from him:

> In the case of proximity, where the danger of losing one's self occurs, the psychological drama becomes one of disentangling the confusions as in *Winter of Artifice* in which the daughter feels in so many ways identified with her father (through love) that she is forced to examine in which way they were not alike... (*Novel of the Future* 71)

Only by seeing the childishness in the father can the daughter set her self free from his influence:

> If she wishes to live, to establish her own autonomous being, the woman must free herself from the bewildering mixture of childish dependence and haughty authoritarianism displayed by her father and, of course, defended in the name of love. (Spencer 71-2)

The daughter realizes she has been "all through the world seeking a father...loving the father...awaiting the father...and finding the child" (*Winter of Artifice* 57). Like Djuna, the daughter creates for herself a fatherless world where she will never encounter such a figure again: "The woman who stands here is not your daughter. It is the woman who has escaped the stigmata of parental love... I stopped loving my father a long time ago. What remained was the slavery to a pattern" (73, 84-5). Her stillbirth at the end of the story is symbolic of the child in her dying and the woman being reborn: "The little girl in her was dead too. The woman was saved. And with the little girl died the need of a father" (86).

One needs to see one's doubles for who they really are to break free of the cycle of the incest family. In *The Four Chambered Heart*, when Djuna accepts Rango and Zora for who they are, rather than who she has tried to make them out to be, she comes closer to a realization of who she are.* Though all of her selves are integrated into one being, she is still many. In "Winter of Artifice," the daughter finally accepts her father's flaws, recognizes them in herself, and is able to overcome them and step out of the Don Juan cycle. She betters herself by accepting her father. Loving others for themselves, rather than loving the self in others, leads to finally accepting and loving the self. Even simply admitting to oneself the narcissistic attraction inherent in the incest family alone seems to offer results:

> Miguel said, "You two are exactly alike."
>
> "But Donald is more truthful," said Elena, thinking how easily he betrayed the fact that he did not love Miguel wholly, whereas she would have concealed this, out of fear of hurting the other. "Because he loves less," said Miguel. "He is a narcissist." A warmth broke the taboo between Donald and Elena, and Miguel and Elena. Love now flowed among the three of them, shared, transmitted, contagious, the threads binding them... Everything was revealed to the naked eye. (*Delta of Venus* 116)

Again, the scene between Djuna and Donald in *Children of the Albatross*, repeats the sentiment:

> Warmth in the air. The spring foliage shivering out of pure coquetry, not out of discomfort. Love flowing now between the three, shared, transmitted, contagious, as if Michael were at last free to love Djuna in the form of a boy, through the body of Donald to reach Djuna whom he could never reach directly... (*Cities of the Interior* 159)

Once this gradual realization occurs, the afflicted, wandering aimlessly in the house of incest, is closer to finding the self in her self, not in twins, doubles or others. Nin's women will only find themselves if they accept themselves as separate beings with many facets. This realization

---

* *The phrase "who she are" is a reference to Hélène Cixous' construct of multiple selves.*

could only be achieved if, rather than project her feelings onto a double, a character makes the journey into herself and realizes that the doubles she has surrounded herself with are composites like herself. Instead of looking to members of an incest family for the answer of how to get in touch with her self, to rebuild the broken bridge with the world, she needs to turn her eyes inward. It is only when Nin's characters step outside of the cycle of the incest family and see it for what it is that they wrench their gaze away from the narcissus pool of the double and heal themselves by looking into the mirror of the self.◈

*Works Cited*

Dubow, Wendy M., ed. *Conversations with Anaïs Nin.* Jackson: University Press of Mississippi, 1994.

Fitch, Noel Riley. *Anaïs: The Erotic Life of Anaïs Nin.* Boston: Little, Brown and Company, 1993.

Nin, Anaïs. *Cities of the Interior.* Athens: Swallow/Ohio University Press, 1980.

----. *Delta of Venus.* New York: Pocket, 1990.

----. *House of Incest.* Denver: Swallow Press, 1958.

----. *The Novel of the Future.* Athens: Swallow/Ohio University Press, 1968.

----. "Sabina." *Anaïs Nin Reader*, Ed. Philip K. Jason. Chicago: Swallow Press, 1973. 32-9.

----. *A Spy in the House of Love.* Athens: Swallow/Ohio University Press, 1959.

----. *Under A Glass Bell and Other Stories.* Chicago: Swallow Press, 1948.

----. *Waste of Timelessness and Other Early Stories.* Athens: Swallow Press/Ohio University Press, 1993.

----. *Winter of Artifice: Three Novelettes.* Denver: Swallow Press, 1961.

Rogers, Robert. *A Psychoanalytic Study of the Double in Literature.* Detroit: Wayne State University Press, 1970.

Sayre, Gary. "*House of Incest*: Two Interpretations." *Anaïs, Art and Artists, a Collection of Essays.* Ed. Sharon Spencer. Greenwood: Penkevill Publishing, 1986. 45-48.

Spencer, Sharon. "Anaïs Nin's 'Continuous Novel' *Cities of the Interior.* Ed. Zaller, Robert. *A Casebook on Anaïs Nin*, New York: Meridian Books, 1974, 65-76.

Young, Elizabeth and Graham Caveney. *Shopping in Space: Essays on America's Blank Generation Fiction.* New York: Atlantic Monthly Press, 1992.

[1] Pierre is institutionalized because of his delusion that all people have doubles:

"The president did not die today," said the doctor.

"Not he, perhaps, but then the other; the one who is like him."

"There is one like him?"

"Yes, just as there is one who is exactly like me, who thinks everything I think, it is a woman, it is my betrothed, but I can't find her."

"Does she know you are here?"

"Not yet."

Pierre tells the doctor he sees "this personage...in the mirror" (*Under a Glass Bell* 55).

[2] Both Michael and Miguel are lovers of Donald. Nin re-uses a scene from "Elena" in *Children of the Albatross*, switching Elena with Djuna and Miguel with Michael. Miguel, being Spanish for Michael, could be the same person, but there are minor differences between the two characters.

[3] Anaïs Nin discussed the scene in an interview: "I spoke of Sabina as being the woman Lillian wanted to be, the free woman. I was trying to separate the elements of genuine lesbianism from the narcissistic love which you see in adolescents. My own experience with this kind of relationship was based on the fact that this was the woman I wanted to be. In wanting to become like the other we sometimes confuse it with love" (Dubow, 124).

[4] In the story, Lillian confronts a therapist about her relationships with women.

[5] The Voice confides to Djuna: "Today I don't know whether this is a healing or a contagion. I am only discovering that we are all alike, and my patients desperately do not want me to be like them" (*Winter of Artifice*, 113).

[6] Nin's therapist, Otto Rank, told her that her own love for June Miller "was not lesbianism...but an acting out of her father's behavior, a Don Juan courting women" (Fitch, 165).

[7] It is unclear, but this interaction between Lilith and the Voice leads the reader to believe that Lilith may be the daughter from the previous novella, "Winter of Artifice."

[8] It is important to note that although many continuing male characters in her novels eschew women to become exclusively homosexual for the remainder of the books, all the characters in Nin's literature that experience lesbianism return to men. It seems as if, since Nin saw homosexuality as immature, that a truly mature woman would not choose to remain a homosexual. Once the growth she sought had taken place, the character returned to less adolescent styles of love. The men in Nin's books do not generally find themselves as often as the woman eventually do.

Kim Krizan

## Anaïs Style

*The birth of a lifelong passion*

Much has been said about "Jackie Style," "Audrey Style," and even "Sophia Style." These women—so famous they are recognized by their first names—are international sartorial icons. But how can one get excited about a pillbox hat or a bateau neckline when one has Anaïs Nin naked from the waist up and with a birdcage on her head? Or wearing a miniskirt and go-go boots at 68? Or gliding along urban streets dressed in flowing gowns and gold slippers? Anaïs Nin's style could knock the Jackies of this world right off their pedestals, and yet her passion for clothing had a painful birth.

An examination of *Linotte: The Early Diary of Anaïs Nin 1914-1920*, which she began at age eleven as a series of letters intended for her father, reveals the inception of lifelong themes. They include Nin's struggle with the intense sorrow caused by her father's abandonment of the family, her painful longing for love, and her worship of beauty. Significantly, Nin's first diary also chronicles the launch of her interest in clothes, an obsession that seemed to grow right along with her writing.

Looking back on her life, Nin said that as a child she realized "life would be more bearable if [she] looked at it as an adventure and a tale" (*vii*). Notably, when her father left Nin's mother, Nin felt that he had left her. She felt betrayed, broken-hearted, and worried that the parting was her fault (64, 85). But as she, her mother, and brothers sailed away from Europe, Nin gradually began transforming her pain. If life was to be a story and she was to be an actor in a drama, she would most certainly need distinctive costumes.

"Today I almost finished my scarf..." (10). This is the very first mention Nin makes of clothing in her diary, and it is recorded in August 1914 while she is on the ship heading for America. Just a few days later, she writes: "My shawl is nearly finished, just one row still to be added. I have decided it will be for Maman because Grandmother can't wear a color like blue" (12). Soon the family arrives in America, and young Nin is overcome with depression. She believes her new home is ugly, but she consciously transforms this perception and thereby begins transforming her life (30). "Work prevents me from having the painful thoughts that I used to have[,]" she explains, and indeed she keeps busy by helping her mother run their household (52). Often she feels intense sorrow and cries, but she tells her diary she is distracting herself with thoughts of a boy and this "calms [her] pain"

(92-3). With remarkable insight, Nin realizes she has developed a method for coping, and she advises her diary: "Close your eyes to ugly things" (107). And so at age eleven, Anaïs Nin has consciously and pointedly decided to give her life over to "dreams" (96).

Soon Nin is worried about her intention to disengage from "reality." She asks herself whether she is

> ...becoming vain and frivolous? Am I full of the wish to be admired? ...I am a little bird, I say, who has neither strength nor energy, no nest, no place where I can lean and learn to be reasonable. My diary will be my anchor and a harbor for my thoughts. (68)

But as the diary reveals, she continues to throw herself headlong into "dreams" and begins designing a beautiful new life.

While settling in America, some of Nin's first expressions of joy describe her clothes. She writes: "I am delighted! Godmother just made me a present of a pretty red flannel kimono. It's so warm, so soft!" (20). Two pages later she records a gift of "4 pairs of long black stockings and one yellow pair" (22). And after a lecture on the life of Marie Antoinette to benefit the children of Brittany, Nin creates a detailed description of the costumes worn by a model during the lecture (31).

And then begins the campaign of Nin's "Maman," one intending, it seems, to give young Anaïs Nin the happy girlhood that had been compromised by her father. On a Friday in February 1915, Nin writes,

> Maman went out with me by myself and bought me some beautiful black shoes with rubber soles to keep me from the damp. I was very pleased and kept looking at them, but Maman hadn't finished. She also bought me a pretty dress in navy-blue serge with light-blue trimming at the neck and a smart white collar. (49)

Nin continues faithfully recording each acquisition: "I received a pretty white jacket from Godmother and a hat for school. Maman is going to buy me another one for dressing up" (60). And then, the arrival of a trunk from rich relatives: "Maman received a trunk full of clothing from Cuba. I received a beautiful pair of shoes and a jar of 'guava cream,' a specialty of Havana" (61-2).

By May of 1915, less than one year after the family's arrival in America, Nin has clearly begun melding the pain of the loss of her father and her love of clothes:

> Two years, two years since Papa left me at Arcachon. A terrible betrayal seized me that day, I have never felt the pain of separation so deeply. Ah, poor Papa, when will you come, when shall I be able to kiss you and carry out my filial duties toward you? The other day I had a visit from a gentleman who is an uncle of one of Papa's pupils; he brought two packages from Papa. What a nice surprise! As soon as he left I opened the first package, a box camera with films for Thorvald, a gold stickpin for Joaquinito and a pretty leather purse with my initials on it for me. I was mad with joy. Dear little Papa, how nice you are! Yesterday Maman bought me a beautiful blue ribbon for my hair and a pair of white shoes. I am so spoiled. (64)

Clothes have become an oasis of pleasure, a substitution for the love of an absent parent.

The list of gifts and acquisitions continues. On Christmas 1915 Nin receives "a paint box and an embroidered collar and cuff set from my aunt, and Maman had given me, the day before, a scarf and a pink cotton bonnet" (101). She reports that on April 29, 1916 she and her mother "went to Franklin Simon and Lord & Taylor where Maman bought me shoes, stockings, ribbons and some other things" (120). And then, Nin prepares for a genuinely special day in June when she will appear as a dancer in a performance about Joan of Arc at the Union Square Theatre. For this occasion, Nin's mother buys her "beautiful patent-leather shoes and silk stockings and gloves" (172). With the arrival of the big day, Nin writes that she had felt disgusted by the performance hall with its odors and atmosphere of "the worst kind who act in vaudeville," but she focuses on her costume:

> ...a little white blouse, a long dark-green skirt with a little black velvet ribbon near the hem, and a black velvet bodice that laced in front. A little black apron made me look like a peasant from Lorraine, which was how I was supposed to look. I let my hair down and put on a white bonnet with a little black velvet ribbon...at one moment I dared to raise my eyes and where the audience was I saw...a big black hole and just a few faces. That's all. The second time, I was braver and I looked: I saw hands applauding. When we left the stage...that vague sound of applause haunted me for a long time. It wasn't for me, it was for all of us, and yet a voice whispered, "You would like that applause for yourself." ...Dearest Diary, isn't that one more sign which should convince me that my vocation is to seek applause? I think so, and I begin to dream again... (172-5)

Beautiful clothing and applause have married in fourteen year old Nin's mind; the pursuit of such pleasures has become a means for easing her loss.

But in spite of these dreams and triumphs, Nin is not a happy girl. A photo of her from around this period reveals an adolescent with long dark hair who wears a black double-breasted coat and knitted stocking cap. What is notable is her serious—even sad—expression (158). But once again, Nin demonstrates she is conscious of her choice to immerse herself in fantasy:

> If by romantic they mean someone who dreams, I am a romantic, but I shall keep it a secret and never dream except with my diary...
>
> Let's quickly take off our crown of dreams, our coat of "what I believe" and put on the dirty apron of "what is happening." (185)

And so Nin continues focusing on what she believes, describing what she wore on her sixteenth birthday:

> A pretty light-blue dress, the shoulders covered with a big piece of blue tulle that made a charming effect. I wore silk stockings and narrow little shoes, also a coral necklace that Maman had given me for the occasion, and my hair was pulled back in a chignon of curls with a narrow blue ribbon around my head. As guests, we had my friends from school and, for the first time, a few young men. Among other things, we pretended to know how to dance and the rest of the party turned into a real dance. I was delighted and I danced a lot. I was spoiled, I received a large number of gifts and compliments. (209)

Around this time, young Nin also seems to become conscious of the wider world of fashion. While walking along Broadway with her friend Frances, she observes the scene:

> I can't describe the men, who were of all ages and dressed every possible way, but the *women*! Heavens! ...We saw all those ladies walking with little tiny steps. They almost all looked like painted dolls. Each was surrounded by several men and they looked terribly artificial. The more extravagantly they were dressed, the more attention they got from the opposite sex, which would stop walking to admire them. (213)

For teenaged Nin, clothes became the occasion. On April 9, 1919, Nin writes: "Maman took me downtown and bought me a pretty serge cape, patent-leather shoes, black silk stockings and gloves, and we came home very happy." Two days later, she records: "I wore my cape and my beautiful new shoes for the first time, which meant that I went to my dancing lesson putting on more airs than usual" (218). On April 18, she writes that "the weather was beautiful today and I took pleasure in letting my cape float in the breeze. It's a feeling that always makes me think of poets. And a cape can make you believe that you are someone powerful like Napoleon, or a queen with a cloak of diamonds and rubies, or just a girl dressed 'in the fashion of France' (as the song says)" (219). Soon after she takes another walk, specifically to see Easter hats: "In the street, all the ladies have new hats, pretty straw hats with flowers, like mine" (220). And finally, because she is going on a horseback riding date with friends, young Nin reveals her main concern to be the clothes she will wear as she describes the rental of her boots and the fact that her mother and aunt help her dress:

> First I put on a linen blouse with a big collar and a black ribbon tied in a bow, then a jacket of light gray "crash," almost white. A pretty little cane completed my disguise... Maman was tying my hair into a bun and putting powder on my face at the same time. But when I was ready, a murmur of admiration ran through the entire family... A horseback ride is like a trip to fairyland... (238)

Nin, amazingly conscious of her purposeful deferment of pain into a desire for admiration, begins to worry:

> One thing weighed heavily on me: I have been very *pleased* about receiving compliments. But the good priest laughed heartily, and told me it was nothing at all. On the contrary, he added, it's quite natural. (229)

Nin observes that she seems to have two faces, two personalities—one is that of her practical, sociable mother, while the other is of her "philosopher" father. She writes, "When I left home, I was powdered, painted and curled, and in the mirror I saw Maman's image. When I came back, I was pale, serious, pensive and tired, and my hair was disarranged, and in the mirror I saw Papa's image" (230).

It becomes obvious that underneath Nin's obsessions and fantasies is an original wound, a wound even greater than the one caused by the separation from her father. In spite of the pretty dresses and the admiration, young Nin begins to touch on her primal insecurity, saying: "But more than ever, when I look at myself in the mirror, I think I look sad because I am not pretty, and sometimes I would really like to be pretty" (241). And so she returns to her preoccupation with clothes:

> It's this evening that I am going to Emilia's and even if it's only one o'clock and we aren't going until 8:30, being a Nin I can't help getting ready well ahead of time. That's why my pink checked gingham dress is swinging on a hanger, my patent-leather shoes are set out next to my pair of black silk stockings, my white gloves are washed, my handkerchief is perfumed (already) and I have in front of me a little pink hat, very soft and very pretty, that Maman bought me a few days ago. (250)

Nin's interest in dress is encouraged and supported by her mother. Nin describes more purchases:

> A pink ball gown with a great deal of tulle and a big rose at the waist, a navy-blue taffeta dress with funnel- or bell-shaped sleeves, an adorable black velvet jacket, two blouses, one made of georgette and the other of pink net, a pink silk skirt to go with the blouses and the jacket, silk stockings, and—I think that's all... [F]or those unaccountable frivolities for a spoiled girl, Maman spent the fabulous sum of $113.75. And an amazing thing! she has no regrets at all. (260-1)

Nin goes on to describe more ways her mother has indulged her, explaining that while she has new silk stockings, everyone else in the family wears old stockings that have holes (306). Nin believes herself to be "extravagant," and writes of an outing: "I was very glad to go to the cinema, if only because I could wear my little velvet hat embroidered with a red rose and my black jacket, which made a stunning outfit. That shows how extravagant I am" (316).

Young Nin, whose life at this point is mainly housework, diary-writing, and fantasy, begins relating strongly to her absent father:

> Once I put on a floppy black bow tie, which is one of the things I love enthusiastically, and Maman told me that Papa never wore anything else—always a floppy black bow tie. That seemed such an amusing discovery, and such a plausible reason for the liking I have for a black bow, that I was delighted. The whole world can make fun of me...but if Papa could wear a big floppy black bow tie, I am proud to share his taste and do the same!!! Hurray for the artist's bow tie! (328-9)

Thus, she begins to identify with her father, to embrace him by means of style.

Nin's father, a pianist and composer, was known to be attractive, fastidious, and self-indulgent. Sharing these traits seems to be a way young Nin can be close to him, and so she continues describing her beautiful attire and appearance:

> ...one of my extravagances was an adorable pink dance dress with a lot of tulle and a beautiful rose at the waist, but really as simple as it is beautiful and original. I wore it last night with silk stockings and black shoes, and a little piece of pink tulle with fringes of little white pearls, but not a single piece of jewelry because it seemed to me the rose was perfect by itself. My hair, which I fixed with Monsita's help, was artistically arranged in a chignon of curls, like the night of Emilia's concert but even better. My dress was so pretty that the whole family and the people in the house came to the room to see it and exclaim over it. (340)

On the next page she tells her diary: "I want to give you the good news that I have finally adopted the serious chignon as my coiffure." And then, nine pages later she confesses:

> If you like, I will frighten you with the price of my new ensemble. Look:

| | |
|---|---|
| 1 Ermine | $40 |
| 1 Velvet Dress | 29.50 |
| 1 coat | 49.50 |
| | $119.00 |

But at the heart of Nin's fascination with style is a feeling of being closed out, barred from the party of life. In October of 1919, she stands in her house and watches people enjoying an elegant party across the street. Interestingly, instead of describing their appearance, she records her own. She is standing, she writes, "in my nightgown and blue slippers, with my hair hanging down and the brush in my hand" (351). She demonstrates an extraordinary awareness of self and continues pointedly making herself the central character in her story, with an emphasis on costume.

Perhaps inevitably, Nin's family experiences a crash in their finances and her mother is terribly worried (355-6). Still, Nin finds another way to pursue her personal agenda, for she can build her dreams with her own hands. In late November of 1919 she writes:

> I have discovered that I can make hats. Last Saturday I took a little black tulle from an old ball gown of Maman's, the helmet of an old hat of Aunt Antolina's, and a blue flower, and I made a hat that I wore to go to Mass. To my great surprise, first Maman, then Aunt Antolina, Aunt Lolita, the neighbors, etc. etc., all told me that it was very pretty and added that they would like to know where I bought it. (383)

After five years, Nin has gained enough confidence to try to woo her father. In a letter to him, she writes: "I already wear my hair in a bun, because I feel so serious... I should be a lady painter because I was born to wear a black velvet coat and the artist's floppy bow tie" (389). But instead of luring her father to America, Nin begins to get attention from American boys. While sledding with friends, a group of young men call her "White Cap" because of her white beret, and invite her to ride with them. The girls who are present seem jealous and Nin overhears one refer to her as "the biggest flirt!" (394). It is obvious young Nin's campaign for admiration is a success.

Finally, Nin's seventeenth birthday arrives on February 21, 1920. Formal portraits are taken and Nin's mother will host a party. In more ways than one, it is Anaïs Nin's "coming out." She has transformed her loss, set the stage for a writing career, and become beautiful and charming. Pain has given her purpose. As she and her mother plan her party, Nin admits that the thing that interests her most "is the dress I will wear!" (403). Her mother selects the dress in secret and when Nin sees it she is delighted. And then Nin reveals the very heart of her psychic wound, the source of all of her creativity, her "raison d'être":

> Dearest diary, I am sure, I know by a million signs, that I am not ugly any more! I have left behind the period of straight hair, unruly locks, shiny nose, sallow skin—in a word, all the horrors and horrible features of a schoolgirl—all that is past... When I was little, I heard Papa say that I was ugly and the idea never left me. I didn't even try to see if it wasn't true until now. (413-4)

Thus, on the occasion of her seventeenth birthday and after almost six years of struggle, Nin has conquered her father. She has proven him wrong, but also become worthy of him. She is a girl so lovely, so charming, so stylish, she is like one glimpsed in fairytales, for she goes on to write: "I wore my fairytale dress, a crown of flowers on a gold ribbon, my shoes with the Louis XV heels..." (465). Anaïs Nin had made her decision, one from which she did not deviate, one she would not abandon. For her it would be dreams and beauty, poetry and love, Grecian gowns and birdcages against the ugliness, miniskirts and go-go boots against time, gold slippers and flowing capes against the ravages of reality. ◈

*Work Cited*

Nin, Anaïs. *Linotte: The Early Diary of Anaïs Nin 1914-1920*. New York: Harcourt Brace Jovanovich, 1978.

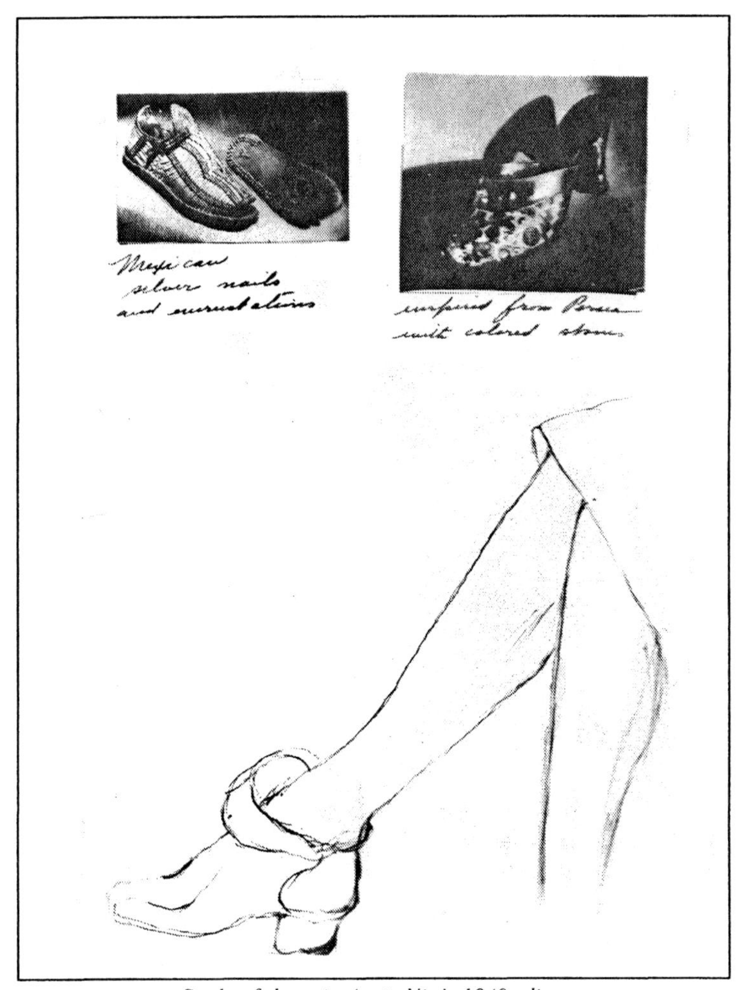

*Study of shoes in Anaïs Nin's 1940s diary*

*Tristine Rainer*

## The Bohemian and the Football Player

*A film treatment on Renate Druks and Ronnie Knox*

*Prologue*

After Anaïs Nin's death in 1977, Renate Druks and I became even closer as friends than we'd been before. In the early 1980s I got into the TV/film business, first as a development exec, then as a producer and writer. I told Renate I could see a film in the story of her love affair with Ronnie Knox, a famous "footballer" (her word). She liked my title "The Bohemian and the Football Player" and became excited. Renate was always game for a creative project, and soon it had mushroomed in our imaginations into a book as well as a film.

"But you have to write the book," Renate said, "I'm not a writer."

"I don't have the time with my job," I declined. I knew, as had Anaïs, that Renate's true gift, given freely to the air, was as a raconteur. "Could you just speak it?" I asked Renate. "Could you tell it to a tape recorder?"

"If I were alone," she considered.

"Could you then transcribe the tapes?" To my surprise and delight, she said she could do that. But not at home. She had recently moved into a cheap Culver City apartment from her house in Malibu. (She'd lost her house in a legal dispute with a contractor she'd hired.) I think Renate really wanted a reason to get out of that shabby apartment. Despite the wall-sized seascape mural she'd painted and hung as her view, she never felt at home there. Also, she wanted to escape the incessant phone calls filtered by her answering machine. They were largely from Ronnie Knox, the love of her life who had later developed mental illness and became homeless.

Renate and I began a routine that lasted for four months. Every weekday at 9 a.m. I would rush down the stairwell of my Miracle Mile apartment in my dress-for-success suit and heels to go to my film development job. A half hour later, Renate, wearing a caftan, would scurry up the stairwell, open my door with the key I'd given her, and read the notes I'd left for her the night before. She would spend the day dictating into the tape recorder I'd set up, then type that day's dictation for my nightly reading.

As if I were her secret confessor, I would never see her, but she would leave for me every night scenes from her life that she had previously believed she could never tell anyone.

The weekend after she wrote "The End" on the last page of the thick manuscript which had accumulated, we cleared away the recorder and typewriter and celebrated with a picnic lunch she'd brought, sitting where the sun streamed in at noon in my otherwise dark apartment.

From her manuscript I wrote the following film treatment. I don't think I ever believed I'd get a movie made from it, but I wanted to reflect back to Renate the inspiration I took from her life.

*The Bohemian and the Football Player*
*Film treatment, originally registered with the WGA, 1981*

This story begins in 1957 when RENATE DRUKS was 38. It is a story of Los Angeles in the '50s. Renate then belonged to a group of American Bohemians and European writers and artists who had settled in Southern California, which included Anaïs Nin, Christopher Isherwood, John Houseman, and film directors James Bridges and Curtis Harrington. Although everyone else in the '50s marched to the same drum, each of these artists lived by their own instrument.

Renate had moved to L.A. from Brooklyn where she'd been married to a successful Jewish doctor with whom she had a son. One day she could no longer live within the constraints of their bourgeois life, so she left with her son, not asking for any money. She set out for the life of a struggling artist. She was painting and working as a hostess at Holiday House restaurant in Malibu when our story begins.

Being free and single, she went out one night with her friend GEMMA to pick up men. They went to the Malibu Sportsmen's Club, frequented by the locals. Sitting at a table with Gemma, Renate exchanged a glance with a young man across the room.

"Change places with me," Renate said to her friend. "Now, before I lose my heart. He's the most gorgeous thing I've ever seen."

Renate and Gemma traded places, but soon the maitre d' came over with a message from the young man, asking Renate to dance.

"If he wants to dance with me, he should come over himself to ask," Renate replied.

"He can't," the maitre d' whispered. "He's a public figure and can't stand a public rejection."

Renate looked at Gemma, resigned, and said, "It's too late." She told the maitre d' to tell the young man she would accept.

RONNIE KNOX (24) came over and Renate suggested to him that he sit down and have a drink with them, "but first you have to show me your I.D. so I can see if you're legally old enough to drink."

When he showed her his driver's license, she was relieved that he wasn't 19 as he looked...still, he was 14 years younger than she. He then peeled out bills from a wad of money to pay for their drinks.

Ronnie, she soon learned, was a famous football player, who had been drafted by UCLA out of high school and gone on to play professionally for the Chicago Bears. He was one of those rare athletes who was all-American, proficient in every sport, and had been pushed by his stepfather to become a super-athlete. He had finally chosen football and, as a star quarterback at UCLA and for the Bears, was famous to everyone but Renate who had never watched football and knew nothing about it.

When Renate and Ronnie rose from the table to dance the sexual electricity between them was undeniable. They all were drinking a lot, and the group decided to go back to Renate's house to have a nightcap. Renate watched Ronnie in his sports car, and could not believe how he drove, drunk, speeding and weaving in and out of traffic on Pacific Coast Highway. When they got to her house, she became very upset with him because he was loud, rowdy, acting like a kid. Her 16 year old son PETER was sleeping in the next room. So she kicked everyone out.

The next morning when Peter came to breakfast he saw an item Ronnie had left. "Who was here?" he asked.

"Ronnie Knox."

"Ronnie Knox was here, and you didn't introduce him to me, Mother!" Peter was about to start college at UCLA. Having been raised by an artist mother and all her artist friends, Peter wanted nothing more than to fit in; to be like everyone else, and so he idolized the all-American Ronnie Knox.

That afternoon Renate and Peter were driving on Pacific Coast Highway, and saw the sports car Ronnie had been driving when he left Renate's. It was perched, leaning over a cliff.

Later, Ronnie, having come to Malibu to retrieve the car, showed up at Renate's door.

The passionate affair they then began was as unstoppable as a tidal wave. Yet it had to be kept secret. Ronnie was engaged to the Rheingold Queen; he had celebrity contracts that required that he maintain the image of a young heartthrob. An affair with a mature, Jewish Bohemian didn't fit the requisite image. For Renate's part, she didn't want her Bohemian friends to know that she was in love with a football player.

For Peter's part, though, he wanted to tell anyone who would listen that his mother's new boyfriend was the all-star Ronnie Knox. Besides, Renate's friends liked and accepted Ronnie, and he certainly liked them. He wanted to be an artist like them; he wanted to be free and

Bohemian like them. He had never wanted to be a sports star; that was his stepfather's dream.

However, Ronnie could not stand up to his stepfather, who tried to control every aspect of Ronnie's life and career. So even when Ronnie and Renate got married, Ronnie kept it a secret and maintained a separate apartment in Santa Monica so that his stepfather would believe that's where he was living alone. Ronnie actually used the apartment as an office where he would go in the afternoons to try to write. He asked Christopher Isherwood for help with his writing. Isherwood encouraged him because he was such a sensitive young man, but Ronnie did not make much progress in his writing.

One day, Renate asked Ronnie to explain football to her. He gave her an example from when he was playing and had hurt his right ankle.

"Here's a riddle," he said. "I had to go out and play so they wrapped up my *left* ankle with bandages. Do you know why they did that?"

Renate could not figure it out. She tried to think of all the koans she knew, but she could not come up with the answer.

"Because the opposition would think it was my left ankle that was injured and that's the one they would attack." So Renate began to understand football.

Another day she and Ronnie were driving into Beverly Hills and they saw a group of people playing football in the park, and Elvis Presley playing with them. Ronnie, who was a huge Elvis fan, said, "Stop the car. I want to go play."

When Ronnie asked to join them they didn't recognize him because he'd grown a beard. They said, "Come on, if you can keep up with us."

Just from watching Ronnie's incredible maneuvers and passes they recognized him, though, because only one person could pass and run that way. Elvis was as excited to be playing football with Ronnie Knox as Ronnie was to meet Elvis. That day Renate saw there were two sides to football, its beautiful, balletic grace, as well as its brutality.

Ronnie thought that if he could be in the right atmosphere, if he and Renate went to Europe, it would inspire his writing. So they made a plan. Because Ronnie had always wanted to sail, they would buy a boat that they would live on, and they would take this boat down the Seine. They would travel and Ronnie would write. However, they didn't have enough money. (Ronnie's stepfather had interfered so much, always negotiating new demands, that the Bears had let Ronnie go.) So Ronnie signed on with a Canadian team, the Argonauts, to play one season for a huge salary. Then he would quit, and with the money he and Renate would follow their plan.

Canadian football is even more brutal than American football, so Ronnie told Renate she couldn't come. He didn't want her to see the violence.

When he came back before finishing the season, he was beat up and injured. He told Renate that they'd wanted him to fix a game, he'd refused to, and so all the guys on the team had beaten him up. But he was there, he had the money, and they were going to Europe.

Renate wanted her son to come with them, but Peter had the opportunity to live with a friend in upscale Pales Verdes, to experience being part of a real American, normal family, and to start college at UCLA, and that's what he wanted to do. So Peter went to pursue the all-American life, while Ronnie went with Renate to pursue the Bohemian life.

Renate negotiated with a Belgian captain, from whom they bought their sailboat, to teach them how to navigate before they set out. But Ronnie didn't really pay attention, so Renate ended up sailing and navigating as well as cooking all their meals and maintaining the boat. Ronnie never even learned how to manage the bilge or the head; he would just pee over the side of the boat. He lived only for the moment. He threw things they needed overboard, made no progress on his writing, and took no responsibility at all. It was Renate's first inkling that there might be a problem with Ronnie. He was not making the transition into being a man, into being independent and taking responsibility for his life. He'd been spoiled as a star athlete and hadn't developed any kind of maturity.

Nonetheless, Renate loved him without reservation, and there were wonderful things that happened on their voyage. Once, because of Ronnie's foolishness, they were headed towards the rapids where the boat was changing locks in the river. The boat was about to go over the edge, and they were headed for disaster and death. Ronnie pulled out a rope and, swinging it like a cowboy, he lassoed the chimney of a house they were passing. Using only that rope, he pulled the boat back from going over the rapids.

They went to Marseilles and then to Spain, still searching for the right atmosphere for Ronnie's writing. In Barcelona, Ronnie, frustrated from rewriting the same page over and over, said he was going to go out for a beer to relax. He did not come home until six the next morning. Renate was so worried that she cried all night. It was but the first of many nights that she would cry and get no sleep. He was out with other women.

They returned to Los Angeles and took a small apartment in West Hollywood. The plan was that Renate would paint, and Ronnie would write. Renate had rented out her house in Malibu, and they lived on that income plus what she could bring in as a commercial artist. However, while she was out and Ronnie was meant to be writing, he would instead get together with friends, hanging out, joking, and at night he would go out with them.

Renate was devastated when she learned that he was messing around with very sexy young women and men and getting into orgies. After her heartbreak, she realized that this was the only way Ronnie could prove himself. He had wanted to become like her and her friends, but he didn't have any of the mental discipline with which to do that. The only thing he had was physical discipline. Proving himself through his physical prowess was the only avenue left to him.

Renate told Ronnie she could not live that way. He would have to get his own place; and they could not live together, but they could part as friends. She even found him a little place in Venice and helped him fix it up. Her heart was aching, but she knew it had to be because she felt so passionately about him. She could not make love with him anymore because it had been so spoiled by the thought of his infidelity. They gave each other gifts when they said good-bye.

In the meantime, Renate's precociously artistic son Peter had quit UCLA and gone to Mexico on a vacation. He hadn't succeeded in making the integration into becoming the all-American boy any more than Ronnie had been able to become an artist. Peter didn't feel accepted at UCLA and became withdrawn. Renate moved back into her Malibu house and Peter moved back in with her, but he was distant and uncommunicative. One evening she came home from work and found Peter unconscious in her living room. She tried CPR, but he was already dead from a heroin overdose. She hadn't even known he had gotten into drugs.

Renate was distraught and hysterical with grief. She could not take care of herself. She couldn't go on living.

Ronnie came to the house and took care of her, spoon fed her, held her hand and let her weep for hours. He kept her from killing herself.

For once, he took on responsibility, for her. He wanted their marriage to work again. They took a trip to Mexico together, but again he could not keep his eyes off the young women and men. Renate could see that though Ronnie had saved her life, their marriage was not going to work, and she returned home, alone.

Renate became a very strong woman. Both men who had depended on her, even lived through her, and whom she loved more than anything in the world, she had been unable to save. But she was going to save herself. She refused to despair. Despite her pain and solitude, she chose to go on and live with engagement, spontaneity, and creativity.

*Epilogue*

Renate was very touched when she read my treatment and that deepened our friendship, though we soon forgot about selling it as a film. Happily, Renate, having picked up the knack for autobiography, continued writing about her life, and no longer needed the aid of a tape recorder. Periodically, she would phone and read to me from her autobiography-in-progress to hear me laugh uproariously.

In exchange for my appreciation of her, Renate was a great boon in supporting me emotionally through my bad and beautiful years in the film business. We suddenly became less close, though, one day in 1987.

By that time Renate had moved from the Culver City apartment to a tiny condo in Hollywood that she'd bought outright for $50,000. Even back in 1987, all she could get for that price was a tiny, nearly windowless, one-room condo on a borderline crowded Hollywood block north of Sunset. Renate faced her moves to reduced circumstances with her characteristic resilience. She brought along the wall-sized, trompe-d'oeil canvases she'd painted, mounted on a roller from which she could unspool a canvas when she wished, as pulling down a portable movie screen. She declared, "Unlike most people, I'm not limited to just one view." She rolled down a seascape when she wanted to calm herself, a mountain vista when she needed relief from the smog, or a Gauguin jungle, replete with wild animals peeking from behind trees, if she felt lonely. She hiked every morning in the Runyon Canyon hills above her congested block, practiced her mantras, played before sleep the self-hypnosis tapes she'd recorded in her own voice to give herself positive thoughts, read her books on Vendanta, and was content. She lived by the credo she and Anaïs subscribed to: Life sets you traps. It's your job to escape them, if only by means of the imagination.

Not that she ever got over the pain of tragically losing the two men she loved. That pain was always peeking through like the creatures in her jungle canvas. And one afternoon, when I'd brought to visit her the 7 year old little girl I was about to adopt, it sprang at me like a jaguar.

I had met Jamie at a home for emotionally troubled children where I'd volunteered as a "special friend." It was the same orphanage, Hollygrove, where Marilyn Monroe had lived as a child. In part, I'd been taken by Jamie's courage and sense of humor as she showed me her five unmatched socks and four worn pairs of panties in the otherwise empty bureau that demarcated her "area" in the dormitory. With pride of possession she also showed me her one toy, a headless Barbie. In part, I was also taken by Jamie's beauty; she had the lanky ease and steady gaze of a young Lauren Bacall. Soon after I'd met her and took her on a shopping outing at the Beverly Center, we were descending on an escalator and a woman ascending on the opposite escalator saw Jamie and gasped, "That is the most beautiful child I've ever seen!"

I'd expected that Renate would be as charmed by this beautiful, neglected child as I was, but that was not her reaction. Renate had prepared tea for us, but when we arrived Jamie wanted none of it because she had spied the dank, unheated swimming pool in the cavernous courtyard of Renate's building, and became obsessed in being allowed to swim there. We let her go in, though she had no swimsuit and had to swim in her underwear. We sat by the side of the pool in the shadowy gloom and watched the child play by herself. When it was time to leave, Jamie, though nearly blue with cold, refused to get out. I took it as any child's love of the water, but Renate became angry. She pulled me aside and hissed, "You don't know what you are doing in adopting this child. You are making a huge mistake!"

At the time I was offended; I thought Renate was being judgmental. Now I see she was trying to protect me. From her experience with rearing a son who developed mental illness and tried to self-medicate with street drugs, she could see, as I could not, the portent of Jamie's oppositional behavior. Renate could also see, as I could not, how much heartbreak I would be bringing into my life and what a toll it would take on me and my dreams.

As I look back, I believe I know why Renate and her best friend Anaïs, and I, their protégée, were blindsided by mental illness in people we loved, why we could not see it for what it was. Each of us in our formative artistic years had been infatuated with Surrealism, its appreciation for and delight in the bizarre mysteries of the unconscious. Renate admired her quiet, artistic son for being different, and when she met Ronnie Knox, she was dazzled by his beauty and strangeness. When Anaïs met June Miller, she was entranced by her mystery as she had been by Antonin Artaud's poetic ravings. When I met Jamie, I was enthralled with her childhood loveliness and quirkiness. We romanticized these people as we romanticized Surrealism, which romanticized mental illness.

Our stories of our beloveds with mental illness, not by accident, resembled the plot of André Breton's iconic Surrealist novel *Nadja.* In it, Breton's narrator walks in a Paris park at dusk where he repeatedly encounters a beautiful, mysterious woman. He begins an affair of the heart with her that consists of watching for her, a few magical conversations with her, and some kisses. The narrator is already possessed with wonder over her when he learns that she is a patient at a nearby mental hospital. The entire encounter is over in ten days, yet the narrator nostalgically romanticizes his *l'Amour Fou* (the title of a later Breton novel). In the last line of *Nadja*, he declares, "Beauty will be convulsive or will not be at all."

Each of us, Renate, Anaïs, and myself, saw the convulsive beauty in our loved ones with mental illness. We were so bedazzled by their mysteriousness that we understood only belatedly that they had an illness. Though Surrealism had given Renate, Anaïs and myself a way to celebrate our lives, a reason to live, in its romanticizing of madness, Surrealism also did us a disservice. Because we were so taken with our loved ones' freedom from commonplace reason and restraint, because we so appreciated their strange poetry, we recognized too late what their sometimes bizarre behavior should have communicated. We were like the people on shore in the Stevie Smith poem who could not hear the message from those at sea in the unconscious: "I was much too far out all my life; and not waving but drowning." ◈

*Ronnie Knox Chicago Bears trading card*

*Dawn Kaczmar*

## A Tragicomic Fact

*It is a tragicomic fact that our proper upbringing has become an ally of the secret police. We do not know how to lie. The "Tell the truth!" imperative drummed into us by our mamas and papas functions so automatically that we feel ashamed of lying even to a secret policeman during an interrogation.*—Milan Kundera in *The Unbearable Lightness of Being*

*I am an excitable person who only understands life lyrically, musically, in whom feelings are much stronger than reason. I am so thirsty for the marvelous that only the marvelous has power over me. Anything I can not transform into something marvelous, I let go. Reality doesn't impress me. I only believe in intoxication, in ecstasy, and when ordinary life shackles me, I escape, one way or another. No more walls.*—Anaïs Nin

My mother told *magnificent* lies.

My mother told magic through lies, enacted sagas through lies, and cultivated friendships through lies. She harbored no remorse for these deceptions; when found out, she did not plead guilty or innocent. She did not plead at all, but smiled, as though you were finally in on her little joke.

*Words. They're plastic, you see*, she cooed to me late at night when she tucked me in. *You form words to your will. There is no real difference between reality and artifice*, as she stroked a loose strand of hair from my forehead. *Everything is creation. We can construct our own fictions.*

We often sat together like this late at night, alone in the dark and whispering. She would explain her soft version of the world to me.

She told me she believed in honesty only as far as it did not exclude fantasy. She said reason and rationality were moveable type and that there was nothing more devilish than the subversion of logic.

She lived for amusement and dominance over her language and others. To conquer, for her, was the birth of creativity, a singularity that, once trespassed, revealed unpredictable and occasionally volatile results. People did not exist in a kingdom of ends, but as potential challenges to overcome by means of seduction. She played with fire by mastery. *I will learn you*, she seemed to say, *and then I will use you, play with you. You will bend to my will.*

I imagined her as the wind, invisibly shaping landscapes and truths. Her presence reached further than her physicality. When she leaned in to kiss me at night, her hair sweeping past my face, her breath on my temple, I thought I would swoon from the enormity of her. Through each gesture she seemed to feign a suggestion, to imply a secret bond. I would trace the embroidery on my blankets, feigning a lack of interest, and her eyes would stare into me, through me, and I would feel my cheeks turn hot as my mother's eyes bore into me.

She taught me this duplicity: that the truth is not a measure of integrity, but an arbitrary perception of incomplete facts. *We are myths*, she said, *we are unscathed by reality*. She took great pains to explain to me that the world ran on the assumption that everyone was telling the truth—that they needed to in order to get on with their day. *They think lies are a form of obstruction and separation. Not you and I*, she would say. *We lie for the sake of fluidity. To forge connections. To protect our freedom.*

*Will they catch us?* I asked her innocently.

*No, dear. We are at an advantage; we lack cause for suspicion. We dance on their presumption. You will never fear lying to the secret police; your heart will beat slow and steady and nothing will give you away. It is our nature to deceive, to weave our fictions imperceptibly into fact.*

She meant for us to feel conspiratorial, but truthfully I feared her. I felt she was capable of anything. My trust in her was plagued with uncertainty; I searched her constantly for lies, for evidence to the contrary. I wanted my mother dearly. I wanted my mother to *be* my mother and this strange desire revealed my distrust, my hesitancy, my separation from her. Her breast was not where I found myself, safe and complete, but searching for the unreliable premise of my mother. I questioned the strength of our kinship. How I wished to be marvelous, how I wished to be close to her, pulled into her world of fantasy, unbound and unscathed. *Teach me your lyricism*, I would plead, in moments of despair, but she would only stroll away, grinning.

Literature was the foundation of her most persuasive arguments. She would muse, quoting Oscar Wilde while gesturing with a wine glass, *People are neither good nor bad, darling, but either charming or tedious. I wouldn't dare measure you by something so common as your principles, but the vastness of your mind and fantasy.* She would toss her head back and laugh, her long neck punctuated by an arching clavicle, her shoulders spilling forward, muscle and bone pulling downward into her draping light blue silk dress. This memory of her is fixated in my mind as if to represent her ideal form: gesticulating, laughing, her wit incising through reason with fantasy, a razor sharp as Occam's.

And her hair. Lies flew from her hair like feathers in mid-flight or mid-fall. Her hair was always wild.

At any given point, her alibi was fiction; her defense the entire history of literature.

She would huff at earnestness and attempts to gain confidence through sincerity. She took it for granted that, within our heart of hearts, we dwell not in peace, but in conflict. Where could truth possibly exist when the most honest expression of any given situation is at least two contradicting impulses—yes and no—resting calmly in a single, cupped hand? At any given moment, she felt impelled in several directions at once. The only way in which she could remain authentic was to commit herself to no one thing, to no one, to no singular idea, to no notion of continuity, to no religion, to no political affiliation, but only to the transitory authority of amusement.

Ultimately, her fictions were a source of protection. She left not a trace of her self anywhere. She told so many stories, so many lies, that her authentic life story was left anonymous among them. No one knew who she was or where she was from. Had she grown up in the Northeast, robbing orchards as a child? Or in Sweden, playing a flute among the icy winds? She adapted her accent to her location. She had no less than thirteen maiden names and a handful of rumored marriages. When certificates would surface, she would only laugh. She would disappear from time to time, rarely even leaving a note. Her desire to defend was entirely inconsistent: she would say nothing; retort with something outrageously and obviously untrue; or else launch into treatises that her behavior was honest and in accordance to the human condition itself; that inconsistency and contradiction were facts—facts hidden under the super-supposition of linear retroactive narratives which were merely pretenses and justifications of current, albeit fleeting, conditions.

*Use or be used*, she used to tell me. *Take or be taken.* Her charm was, to her, a power she exerted over others, who carried on unaware that any transaction had taken place. I understood that she always wanted the best for me. *People will do as much as they can get away with,* she said, *and I am skilled at getting away with things.*

In elementary school, our teacher asked us all to invite our parents to come in and give presentations about their professions. It occurred to me then that I had no idea what my mother did, how she made money, or how we survived. I never once saw her take a job. When I asked her that night, she laughed, always she laughed: *Work? Darling, we're privately funded. People will pay us just to breathe. Didn't you know? Silly girl.* We were then assigned to write an essay about our parents. I received an *F* on my essay for my rather brief explanation of my mother's profession: *She breathes. Exquisitely.*

She would pet my head softly, hush my sobs after she had been away for a long interval, and whisper to me, *My darling, my darling, don't you understand? You and I, we do not live by obligations, not even to each other. You will abandon me in old age as I abandon you now. We live for the marvelous, for the fantastic, not the banal. We transcend commitment. Doesn't it make you laugh, my love?*

For a while, I would burst into tears every time I saw her leaving the apartment, fearing that it would be another long absence, or that she would not come back at all. She would lean down, kiss my forehead, and say, *You will forgive me*, before turning on her heel and leaving, her hair flying like a pack of hornets behind her. *You will forgive me and you will thank me. You will grow immune to cruelty. You will grow triumphant.*

During my late teens, my mother had taken a semi-stable lover—more stable, at least, than any other I had ever witnessed. He was younger than she, but just as quick and just as cruel. We would speak briefly sometimes, but nothing beyond the basic requirements of politeness. Through these pleasantries, his eyes would flit leisurely across my body with such utter lack of concern that it set me on fire. He made no excuses for himself. *Yes, I can see why mother loves you*, I thought.

My shock at this behavior was measured through stiffness: I could not be natural around him. Once he caught onto this fact, he seemed to taunt me with it. He seemed to tease me with rudimentary exchanges, as if it were merely a pretense. He seemed to tempt me with the mundane, daring me to identify or acknowledge what tacitly existed between us. He spoke to me only through suggestion, only through subtleties and inflections. He would pick the dullest topic imaginable with which to provoke me.

"Wasn't your mother's toast delicious today?" he would ask. My mother would hum to herself, distracted with the compliment.

"Yes, it was," I would respond, my eyes cast down.

"How do you think she makes such delicious toast?" He would smile and suppress a laugh as I struggled to explain the intricacies of our toaster. "Oh, really? Tell me *more*," his voice would curl.

He seemed to moan louder than necessary when coupling with my mother. I heard his voice echoing through the stone halls of our house, moving into my bedroom and compounded with a cold rush of wind tunneling throughout the chambers, rattling me, chilling me. When I would see him the next morning at breakfast, he would lean back in his chair, his legs stretched before him, and look at me as though he were waiting for me to crawl into his lap and kiss him around the neck, to beg for him, and attempt to procure the moans from the night before.

I assume this, because on a morning when my mother rushed quickly out of the house for an appointment, leaving him behind, this is precisely what transpired. We sat across from each other in the living room, each absorbed in a book when, at some seemingly arbitrary moment, he placed his book down next to him on the table. He folded his hands and quietly looked at me, and said: *Come.*

Without questioning him, without imploring further into what he could have meant, I went to him. I stood before him, peering down into his eyes in silence. *Undress*, he whispered. My dress fell to the floor in one swift gesture. *Sit*, he said, and I folded myself up into his lap, reaching under his shirt collar, exhaling into his neck. His hands moved into my hair. *You are so strange*, he whispered as my head became heavy in his palm.

I closed my eyes. *Yes. I know.*

*There is so much sadness in you.*

I sighed, relieved and resigned with this acknowledgement. *Yes. I know.*

*Your face is so dark and intense. Your eyes are like emptiness. It perverts your innocence. Your pallor straddles fairness and death.*

I said nothing. My identity was such a long-shadowed footnote to my mother's that I rarely even considered it. She was jovial where I was sullen. My silence was hardly palpable in her throaty, guttural laugh. One could feel the intensity and heat of her blood where I was oddly anemic and cold.

We continued to caress and pet each other silently as I sat naked on his lap, our eyes closing, our hands moving unconsciously. I moved my cheek against his and felt him breathing in my thick, black hair, a wad of it clenched in his fist, his breath tickling my ear.

*You are so delicate. I want to lick your perversity*, he said finally.

I sank into him. *You do?*

*Yes*, he groaned and bit into me.

To know oneself through the other. To catch light of one's self through the discrepancies mirrored back, not in unison, but subtle clamors. Having succumbed to my mother's inverted absolutism, I caught myself in the slight disturbances of a new world with which to define my own edges. If it was true that I was my mother's shadow, my own silhouette lay its roots in that moment, spreading like an invasive species, groaning and pulling at its own weight by force of will until material began to spring from its primordial negative space.

And so now, as I stand before her, with my lying harlot eyes and tell her *No, Mother, I did not steal your lover, but oh, my, is he marvelous. Are you not triumphant, Mother? I'm not a liar, I'm merely clever, I'm merely bound by lyricism,* can you truly blame me? ◈

---

*"Love" (digital photography and charcoal) by Colette Standish*

*Colette Standish*

## A Letter

It's been a while
The last time was in a dream
The café on the corner of Rue de l'Abbaye
We talked and talked
Red wine intoxicating every word
Your eyes like diamonds
shone in the dark night of your hair
Hues of blue and purples surrounding you
I was in love
Still am
From the moment we met through the pages of Venus
I was captivated
I was seventeen
you ageless
You touched my heart
and claimed it

So what news?
Did I follow your path?
Yes and no.
The dreams, the laughter,
The tears cried a thousand times
Could have been yours
but they were mine

Seeking answers to life's questions
in the books you left behind
I broke out of my shell
Your silken trail left me
in a state of hallucination.

I took elements from you
and added them to the alchemical process
that became me
Your words
Stardust on paper
Became abstract colours on canvas for me
Your calm, my fire
Your fire, my calm.

Photos taken on a journey
Black and white mirrors
Reds
Ochres
Purples and blues
Hints of green
A Spanish dancer
An incandescent jewel
skimming down the Seine
Each bridge a different lover.
Music follows you
French
Spanish
Arabic
Movements and rhythms flood your body
echoing the river you dance down
Gifts from the lovers you leave behind

I watched you from a distance of years
knowing one day our paths will cross
On an astral flight
I will know you straight away
Diamond eyes
Reflected on ebony seas
Hands touch
Connection
Eruptions crash silently
Explosion of colours
For a brief moment
the sun and the moon
together
guard their children
Sisters
Then it's over
Me to earth.
You the cosmos

The sensual touch of fur on pale skin
The smell of sex laced with incense
lingers in a Souk far away
Could have been your dream
but it was my experience
Visions sketched in my mind
cross deserts dotted with shamans and nomads
to land at your feet by the ocean.

The dream is fading
You whisper your goodbyes
through the photos of my memory
the mirror closes in
Teardrops
dissolve your face into a thousand shimmering lights
Like Japanese lanterns
they glide down the midnight river
As the ripples of time slow down
the water clears and all I see
is me
a reflection
of you.

## Reviews and other items of interest

*Stage review*

**Anaïs: An Erotic Evening with Anaïs Nin**
*A review of the play, written and directed by Michael Phillips*

*Anaïs: An Erotic Evening with Anaïs Nin* is a fictional imagining of what might have happened during one summer weekend in 1954, which Nin apparently does not document in her *Diary*. Writer and director of *Anaïs*, Michael Phillips, imagines that Nin (played by Sonia Maslovskaya, the lone actor in this one-woman show) is called to visit June Mansfield Miller in an Arizona psychiatric hospital. While there, she attempts to seduce the doctor under whose care June recovers from her suicide attempt, and communicates with Henry Miller from across a great distance as if he were standing right before her. The three other characters in the play (June, Henry, and the doctor), rather than being physically present on stage, are conjured in the imagination of the audience through Phillips' writing and through the gaze and gestures of Maslovskaya.

It is shocking—and even a bit disturbing—the weight this one weekend has in Phillips' overall impressions of Nin's life. What is fact and what is fabrication already stands as a contentious matter in Nin scholarship. While the show makes explicit from the start the fictional nature of this story, making work that directly addresses this theme is audacious (and perhaps also a little refreshing) despite the presumptuousness toward which creative work on Nin often tends. Biographical accuracy notwithstanding, because Nin is a lover of theater and all things dramatic, a play seems a fitting form for this comment regarding fact/fiction to take.

Of course, we can never know whether Nin herself would have found this show to be amusing, flattering, insulting, etc. We can only imagine—and imagination is the key ingredient in this show—whether or not these representations of Nin do justice to her fearless and utterly unapologetic way of living.

Red light illuminates a corner of the stage where a chair, small wooden desk, and glass of water wait at the beginning of the show. The Sherry Theater in North Hollywood, being a small space, lends itself to a feeling of intimacy—the audience seems to huddle in the seats, which are so close to the stage we could all but extend our desirous hand for the player to touch.

But while the physical space of the theater evokes intimacy—a sense which stems from close proximity, a magnified need to reach out, to touch and to be touched—the show itself cannot sustain this intimacy and instead vacillates between fostering a feeling of connectivity (or at least the possibility of connectivity) and isolation. Throughout the show Nin fidgets inside the confines of an invisible encasement—the encasement of her past, her memory, her desire—without the ability to connect with actual people (arguably, aside from the audience).

On one hand, the absence of other bodies on stage seems to make space for audience members to fit themselves into the narrative of the show and into Nin's world. On the other hand, because of her encasement, the audience watches Nin struggle and perform a kind of insanity, attempting to make contact with other people in vain. This futility is characteristic of so many critics' and fans' attempts to connect with Nin through her writing.

I use the word "insanity" here very deliberately not just because the play is set in a psychiatric hospital. While we are told Nin is called there to visit June, a resident of the hospital after her attempted suicide, watching Nin bounce around the confines of the stage, literally talking to herself for forty-five minutes straight, throughout the course of the show the audience is taught that it is not June, but rather it is Nin herself who is crazy. Nin chats with the invisible doctor as if in casual confession as she recalls her past exploits with June and Henry, and laments the insufferable complicity and indecision of her husband, Hugo.

*Sonia Maslovskaya as Anaïs Nin. Photo: Ron Yungul*

One cannot ignore the problem of setting this show—about a woman artist who has been so vehemently indicted for being a calculating, mind-game-playing, femme fatale, a snake—in a nut house. That this is a one-woman show, wherein Nin stews in her own memories so deeply she hallucinates Henry's presence, only highlights this glaringly misguided (and some might argue downright offensive) choice, which is sure to drive feminists—at least *this* feminist—mad. The unintentional misogyny in this aspect of the play exists in the unexamined cultural and historical mores about women writers, what it means to be a "good woman," and how we define "insanity"; a male writer who goes mad is labeled "tortured genius," while a woman writer who goes mad is "hysterical." Furthermore, at the time this weekend supposedly went missing in 1954, Nin would have been 51 years old and—even after her plastic surgery—did not bear the taut-muscles and wrinkle-free fresh-face of Maslovskaya, who played her.

In a post-show interview, Phillips talks about wanting to avoid the common perception of Nin's life as glamorous by setting the play in an ambient café reminiscent of those in which she spent hours arguing, dreaming, and philosophizing with Henry Miller, Lawrence Durrell, et al. So rather than glamorizing Nin's life in attempt to avoid a cliché, instead, Phillips frames her as completely off her rocker. And why the cast of one? Phillips expresses his desire to let Nin "speak for herself," something critics/fans/adversaries don't normally do. Ironically, it is not Nin speaking at all, but Phillips, a further reiteration of the impossibility of knowing a Truth about Nin and a boon to the critical argument that Nin's work is "in the eye of the beholder." In fact, in the show, Nin's character observes that June does not exist at all, that she only exists in other people's love for her. Over the course of the show, however, it becomes apparent that this is the very argument Phillips makes about Nin: he positions Nin *as* June—as insane, as seductive, as heedless—and puts her before a desirous audience in order to make her shudder alive.

It is a risky business making creative work based on Anaïs Nin's life and writing; an artist who broaches Nin's life with a creative lens is sure to meet harsh reactions from Nin lovers and critics not necessarily because the work is "good" or "bad," but rather because Nin herself is the subject with whom critics and lovers contend. The complexities and subtext of this show stem almost exclusively from the choice to have a cast of one, namely in the tendency this show has to seduce the audience into a feeling of intimacy, only to remind us—sometimes gently, sometimes coldly—that Nin can never be truly touched. Within this play, between intimacy and repulsion, is the most accurate reflection of Nin I could imagine. *Anaïs: An Erotic Evening with Anaïs*

*Nin* is a valiant attempt even as it requires, at best, a suspension of belief, and at worst, an agreement to suspend your misogyny sensor. ◈
***—Sarah B. Burghauser***

*Music review*

**As We Are** by Pam Shaffer, 2010, CD/download.
*A mini-review of the album and comments from the artist, Pam Shaffer.*

Anaïs Nin's life and work have inspired other artists to create paintings, sculptures, films, plays, and books. Now we can add an entire album of music to the list. Pam Shaffer, a Los Angeles based singer-songwriter, has just released her first full length album based on Nin's Paris diaries, entitled *As We Are* (culled from the famous Nin quote, "We don't see things as they are, we see them as we are") which includes the songs "Henry," "Gonzalo," "Hugh," "June," "Nanakepichu," among others.

With her timeless musical arrangements and knowing lyrics, such as those of "June," *Your bracelets weigh heavily on my wrist / They jangle and they pull / On my delicate hands like you pull on my heart with your / Tangled words your dancer's legs / Kick through my thoughts battering out all my sense of / Doubt of the longing I feel when you leave / That careless hole I see on your sleeve / June June June / You're like a heady perfume / June June June / I'm drowning in you*, Shaffer has captured the Nin aura musically. That said, this is an album that will appeal to music fans in general as well as Nin fans; in other words, it is not a narrowly rendered work that will exclude much of the listening audience, but a well-crafted, cohesive collection of songs in the indie spirit. Instead of excluding listeners, it will, if anything, encourage them to unravel the meaning of the songs by exploring the source of their inspiration.
***—Paul Herron***

Shaffer was asked to comment on her album; her thoughts follow:

I have played the piano for just about as long as I can recall and wrote my very first song about a baby falling out of a tree (rather derivative in retrospect and an odd commentary on children's songs). Music was always my favorite mode of expression but I also painted a fair amount as a child and enjoyed writing poetry as an adolescent.

There's a line in a Jewel song that says, *You can be Henry Miller and I'll be Anaïs Nin / This time it will be even better we'll stay together in the end.* I remember hearing that line and wondering who those people were. Though my interest was piqued, it took me a few years to actually buy and read *Henry and June*. By the time I was 18, I had read it through several times and had moved onto her other diaries along with some of her essays. Reading her words was much like seeing my own thoughts committed to paper though they were ideas I had never dared to have before. I read her work consistently through college and wrote my independent honors thesis about how her life and art merged in an ideal state in the 1930s.

Anaïs's life and work has affected me in a myriad of ways. Artistically, she has shown me that I must persevere and work within my own style whether it is popular or not. She writes in such a particular voice and does not stray from her own intuitive expression. She was not "successful" as a writer for much of her life, but she kept writing regardless. Her style is beautiful and accessible to me, but it might not be to others. She made her life into her art, which inspires me greatly. Though I do not always agree with the choices she made in her life, it is illuminating to read about her successes and failures as she attempted to live her life to its fullest degree. Her work reminds me not to settle for half-measures and to pursue my passions with all my energy. Clearly, her writing greatly influenced my own as I love the fluidity of her prose and the way she lets her stories unfold. I strive to write songs that operate the same way, utilizing the unconscious material and blending it with the conscious content.

A few years ago, the song "Henry" simply popped into my head. I wasn't setting out to write a song about Anaïs and Henry, but there it was. It stood out quite a bit from the rest of my material, which was mostly drawn from my own life. I started to think that perhaps Henry was "lonely" and that I should write about June. Having written a thesis on Anaïs's diaries, the source material was fresh in mind. Over the course of two years, I wrote all of the songs for the album. At the time, I was also writing songs about myself and other topics, but the Anaïs songs tended to have a distinct feel to them, a cohesive character that set them apart from my other work. I had an inkling that they were meant to be a concept album, and by the time I was mixing my previous EP, I was talking with my producer about recording the Anaïs songs together as an album. We began recording demos based on my sketches from my laptop recordings in early 2009, and that was the genesis of the album. My source materials span her dairies and unexpurgated works from 1930-1938, though I have also read *House of Incest* along with *Cities of the Interior*, so you never know what might have snuck in there.

In a way, her most famous quote was a perfect album title, because each of the songs is a different character. The songs are coming to the listener as "they" are, and each listener will take something different from them, thus fulfilling the concept of the quote. I think that quote is universal and insightful but was far too long for an album title. "As We Are" can be interpreted in many ways, but I hope it accurately depicts the nature of the album.

I recall telling my friend Karin Tatoyan about my idea for an Anaïs Nin concept album while sitting outside the Echo Curio on the curb of Sunset Boulevard in Echo Park. She herself is an astonishingly talented musician, and she looked at me with wide eyes and said my idea was brilliant. I laughed and recounted how hard it was to find a thesis advisor because none of my professors were versed in the works of Anaïs Nin and that I couldn't have possibly found a more obscure topic about which to write. She told me that very few people would have a clue what I was doing, but those who did would be thrilled, and those who did not would at the very least be intrigued by such a mysterious subject. Writing an album about Anaïs Nin matches the general theme of my life, which continuously reveals that I am quite good at accomplishing unusual, eccentric tasks but mediocre at best when it comes to easy and practical ones. I was always the kid who could do a one-handed cartwheel but might stub my toe while walking in my own room. I could solve an algebraic equation in my head but I might not count our change correctly. I am aware that I likely should have written or released a more general album first, one that was perhaps more easily relatable and accessible to draw people in before I delved into the unknown. However, I've never done things the easy way, and at least now my listeners will be those who will hopefully follow me down dark paths as well as well-lit ones. ◈

---

*The album can be sampled and bought at http://pamshaffer.bandcamp.com/.*

**Introduction to *The Portable Anaïs Nin***

*Introduction to and table of contents of* The Portable Anaïs Nin. *Edited and introduced by Benjamin Franklin V. Sky Blue Press, 2010.*

Anaïs Nin was never more popular than in the early and mid 1970s. After decades as an all-but-ignored fiction writer, she gained acclaim with the publication of the first volume of her diary in 1966. As more volumes appeared, her recognition increased, both because of the nature of the books and because their publication more-or-less coincided with the rise of second-wave feminism. Many readers viewed Nin as an idol, as the ultimate woman, as one who apparently succeeded in a man's world on her own terms. She lectured at colleges and universities, where her books were taught; was interviewed frequently; corresponded voluminously; wrote blurbs for and introductions to other writers' books. She received scholarly attention through articles and monographs. Her fame spread: her books were published in England, and elsewhere in translation. In 1973, the publisher of Nin's fiction, the Swallow Press in Chicago, acknowledged Nin's reputation by publishing *Anaïs Nin Reader*, which contains selections from Nin's published writings. By then, all the fiction Nin intended for publication had been published, as had her criticism; four volumes of the diary were in print. From this material, the editor of the *Reader*, Philip K. Jason, a major Nin scholar, made judicious selections. Since the publication of his book, however, the number of Nin titles has approximately doubled, with eleven new volumes of the diary and two books of erotica being most important. Now, the time seems right for another sampling of Nin's work, not only because of the existence of this new material or because almost forty years have passed since the publication of Jason's book, but also to encourage a reconsideration of Nin's writing, which no longer attracts the dedicated readership it did in 1973.

In 1914, at age eleven, Nin began keeping a diary as a letter to her father, who had abandoned the family; she continued it for the remainder of her life. From this enormous document, Harcourt ultimately published fifteen volumes, the first two in conjunction with the Denver publisher Alan Swallow. All are represented here by selections that present a complete event or scene. In these excerpts, Nin writes about family members, friends, analysis, sex, abortion, music, dancing, writing, and death, among other topics.

The diary occasionally presents two versions of events. This is so because sensitive material omitted from the first two volumes (1966,

1967) is included in the posthumously published diaries covering the years 1931-1939, books presented as "unexpurgated." These later books (*Henry and June* [1986], *Incest* [1992], *Fire* [1995], and *Nearer the Moon* [1996]) were published specifically to present the previously withheld material. For episodes published in substantially different forms, I use the "unexpurgated" versions. For example, I include a selection about Nin and June Miller (dated January 1932) from *Henry and June*, which mentions Nin's husband, Hugh Guiler, and her cousin, Eduardo Sánchez, instead of similar material (dated 31 December 1931) from *The Diary of Anaïs Nin, 1931-1934*, which does not.

The word "unexpurgated" suggests completeness, openness, frankness. Indeed, the four volumes of the diary so identified include graphic descriptions of the author's relationships, most notably with Henry Miller and Nin's father. Forthright though these revelations seem, they might not be as complete or accurate as "unexpurgated" implies. This possibility exists because, as biographer Deirdre Bair notes, in 1920 Nin "began a lifelong pattern: as she wrote new [diary entries], she constantly revised the old." Bair also observes that in the 1940s, Nin rewrote all the diaries, an action that constituted her "first consistent and complete reinvention of her past."[1] This is not to say, though, that the diaries—expurgated or unexpurgated—are untrue either in their general depictions of events or emotionally. Rewriting need not alter basic truths.

Two principles governed the selecting of fiction for this book: I wanted entire works or complete sections of books rather than a few pages from here and there, and I desired pieces that represent Nin at or near what I think is her best. *The House of Incest*, her first book of fiction, is, in my judgment, her most accomplished one, so I include it. How to represent Nin's erotica, written in the early 1940s but not published during Nin's lifetime? Because some of the diary selections included here have strong sexual content and I do not wish to overemphasize this aspect of Nin's work, I reproduce one of the shortest erotic stories, "Manuel." From the non-erotic short fiction, I include "Houseboat," the initial story in *Under a Glass Bell*, not only because of its position in the book, but also because it continues the theme of *House of Incest*, which is a major theme in her fiction generally: the impulse to live apart from reality leads to a living death and therefore must be resisted.[2] Inspired by the author's experiences on a houseboat on the Seine, the story illustrates Nin's use of diary material as a source for fiction. After "Lillian and Djuna" appeared as a novella in *This Hunger* (1945) and as the second part of *Ladders to Fire* (1946), Nin changed its title to "This Hunger" for the English edition of *Ladders to Fire* (1963) and made it the opening section of the novel. I include "This Hunger" because of its prominent place in Nin's continuous novel and because it primarily concerns Lillian, on whom Nin focuses at the end of *Seduction of the Minotaur* (1961), which concludes the continuous novel.[3] Lillian frames the whole. Like "Lillian and Djuna"/"This Hunger," "Stella" appeared in *This Hunger* and *Ladders to Fire* (as the first part) before being repositioned. In 1961, Nin placed it in *Winter of Artifice*, where it remains. I intend "Stella" to serve as an example of a Nin novella.

Nin wrote non-fiction prose of a critical nature. Her two earliest mature publications focus on D.H. Lawrence: a 1930 article in *Canadian Forum*, where she uses the pseudonym Melisendra, and *D.H. Lawrence: An Unprofessional Study* (1932). Later, she addressed issues relating to the writing of fiction in the essays *Realism and Reality* (1946) and *On Writing* (1947) and discussed contemporary authors in *The Novel of the Future* (1968). Here, I represent this aspect of Nin's writing with the two essays published in the mid 1940s because they express, succinctly, her literary attitudes at the beginning of her career as a novelist.

During the last decade of her life, Nin was interviewed many times, and interviews were published in such places as *Mademoiselle*, *Vogue*, *The Los Angeles Times*, *The San Francisco Chronicle*, and *Chicago Review*. Wendy M. DuBow collected some of them in *Conversations with Anaïs Nin* (1994). Nin's comments about writing make the interview included here, conducted by Duane Schneider and absent from DuBow's book, particularly valuable.

Before each selection, I provide its context or indicate its subject. Following almost every non-fiction selection, I identify people, publications, and artistic works to which Nin refers. Treating such information in a paragraph avoids the cumbersomeness of using many footnotes in short selections. Also with the non-fiction, I translate words, phrases, and sentences that are written in languages other than English, with the exception of those commonly understood and, usually, those for which Nin's texts provide translations. In my comments about the non-fiction, I include diacritical markings when called for (as with Joaquín), though—believing in the sanctity of the text—I do not add diacritics to Nin's texts (Joaquin).

I use the text of the last American edition of works published during the author's lifetime because it presumably represents Nin's final textual preferences.[4] Two selections, the prologue to *Ladders to Fire* (1963) and the preface to *Under a Glass Bell* (1968), were published only in England. I use the 1968 version of the latter because while it was edited for inclusion in the collection published by Penguin in 1978, I cannot determine if Nin, who died in 1977, made the changes. With works published posthumously, I use the first editions.

In his *Reader*, Jason provides a section of Nin's fiction and another of non-fiction. With a few exceptions, I arrange the contents of this book chronologically, regardless of genre, from a 1915 diary entry about Nin's parents to one about death (1975-1976). (Dates Nin gives to diary entries might not always be accurate.) Such an arrangement permits the charting of Nin's interests and attitudes, themes and techniques, from age twelve to her early seventies. The exceptions are these: with "Manuel," I add two comments Nin composed about writing erotica, one from near the end of her life; with "Houseboat," I provide Nin's statements from 1944 and 1968 about *Under a Glass Bell*, of which "Houseboat" became a part; with "This Hunger," I include Nin's 1946 and 1963 prologues to *Ladders to Fire*, as well as the 1974 preface to *Cities of the Interior*, because they deal with Nin's continuous novel, which "This Hunger" introduces. ◈

***—Benjamin Franklin V***

*Notes*

[1] Deirdre Bair, *Anaïs Nin: A Biography* (New York: Putnam's, 1995), 76, 279.

[2] For vague, unconvincing reasons, Gunther Stuhlmann, Nin's agent, rearranged the contents of *Under a Glass Bell* in 1995, despite Nin's long-held belief that her sequence of stories was as she desired it. At the time of this writing, 2010, Stuhlmann's arrangement of the stories, which places "The Labyrinth" first, remains in print with Swallow Press/Ohio University Press. For a discussion of the positioning of stories in Nin's collection, see Benjamin Franklin V, "Noli Me Tangere: The Structure of Anaïs Nin's *Under a Glass Bell*," *Studies in Short Fiction* 34 (Fall 1997): 459-79. "Houseboat" is the only work present in both Jason's *Reader* and this book; although the earlier volume includes excerpts from *House of Incest*, the prose poem is published here in complete form.

[3] Nin's continuous novel includes *Ladders to Fire* (1946), *Children of the Albatross* (1947), *The Four-Chambered Heart* (1950), *A Spy in the House of Love* (1954), and *Seduction of the Minotaur* (1961). The final novel was originally *Solar Barque* (1958), the text of which Nin expanded and titled *Seduction of the Minotaur*. She published the novels in one volume as *Cities of the Interior* in 1959, with *Solar Barque* as the last novel, and again in 1974, with *Seduction of the Minotaur* replacing *Solar Barque*.

[4] To identify various editions of Nin's books published during the author's lifetime, see Franklin, *Anaïs Nin Character Dictionary and Index to Diary Excerpts* (Troy, MI: Sky Blue Press, 2009), 62-65.

**Table of Contents of *The Portable Anaïs Nin***



---

*Internet*

**Anaïs Nin Trust Online Bookstore**: An online bookstore from which titles can be purchased that are certified to have belonged to the Silver Lake house collection assembled by Anaïs Nin and Rupert Pole, including several out of print rarities: www.anaisnintrust.org.

**Anaïs Nin e-bookstore**: An updated list of all digital Nin titles: http://anaisninblog.skybluepress.com/2010/10/anais-nin-e-bookstore/

**The Official Anaïs Nin Blog**: A frequently updated site with biographical facts, information, and bibliography relating to Anaïs Nin and her circle: http://anaisninblog.skybluepress.com

**Anaïs Nin on Twitter**: Updates on Nin and her circle in 140 characters or less: http://twitter.com/anaisninblog

**The Cosmodemonic Telegraph Company: A Henry Miller Blog**: A blog concentrating on biographical and bibliographical facts related to Miller: http://cosmotc.blogspot.com

**Walking Paris with Henry Miller**: A site devoted to Miller's years in Paris, with photos, maps, anecdotes: http://www.millerwalks.com

**International Lawrence Durrell Society**: The most comprehensive Durrell site on the web: http://www.lawrencedurrell.org

**Maya Deren Forum**: A forum with a biography and filmography; links to films and other publications: http://www.algonet.se/~mjsull/

**Beatrice Wood Center for the Arts**: A site dedicated to the art center that was inspired by Wood; with a biography and links to workshops and exhibitions: http://www.beatricewood.com/biography.html

**Philip Kaufman**: The *Henry & June* director's official web site: http://www.philipkaufman.com

**List of available digital Anaïs Nin titles:**

Anthology:
*The Portable Anaïs Nin* (Sky Blue Press)

Diaries:
*Diary of Anaïs Nin Vol. 2* (Houghton Mifflin Harcourt)
*Diary of Anaïs Nin Vol. 3* (Houghton Mifflin Harcourt)
*Diary of Anaïs Nin Vol. 4* (Houghton Mifflin Harcourt)
*Diary of Anaïs Nin Vol. 5* (Houghton Mifflin Harcourt)
*Fire: From "A Journal of Love"* (Houghton Mifflin Harcourt)

Erotica:
*Delta of Venus* (Houghton Mifflin Harcourt)
*Little Birds* (Houghton Mifflin Harcourt)

Fiction:
*Children of the Albatross* (Sky Blue Press)
*Collages* (Sky Blue Press)
*The Four-Chambered Heart* (Sky Blue Press)
*House of Incest* (Sky Blue Press)
*Ladders to Fire* (Sky Blue Press)
*Seduction of the Minotaur* (Sky Blue Press)
*A Spy in the House of Love* (Sky Blue Press)
*Stella* (Sky Blue Press)
*Under a Glass Bell and Other Stories* (Sky Blue Press)
*The Winter of Artifice* (Sky Blue Press)

Scholarship:
*A Café in Space: The Anaïs Nin Literary Journal 6* (Sky Blue Press)
*A Café in Space: The Anaïs Nin Literary Journal 7* (Sky Blue Press)

For a continually updated list, visit:
http://anaisninblog.skybluepress.com/2010/10/anais-nin-e-bookstore/